WE REAL cOOL

WE REAL COOL

Black Men and Masculinity

bell hooks

Routledge
Taylor & Francis Group
New York London

Published in 2004 by
Routledge
Taylor & Francis Group
270 Madison Avenue
New York, NY 10016
www.routledge-ny.com

Published in Great Britain by
Routledge
Taylor & Francis Group
2 Park Square
Milton Park, Abingdon
Oxon OX14 4RN
www.routledge.co.uk

Routledge is an imprint of the Taylor & Francis Group.

© 2004 by Gloria Watkins

Printed in the United States of America on acid-free paper.

Library of Congress Cataloging-in-Publication Data

hooks, bell.
    We real cool : Black men and masculinity / bell hooks.
       p. cm.
    Includes index.
       ISBN 0-415-96926-3 (HB : alk. paper) — ISBN 0-415-96927-1 (pbk. :
    alk. paper)
    1. African American men—Social conditions. 2. African American
    men—Social life and customs. 3. African American men—Psychology. 4.
    Masculinity—United States. 5. Sex role—United States. 6. United
    States—Race relations. I. Title.
    E185.86.H7417 2003
    305.38'896073—dc22   2003016951

i was not meant to be alone and without you who understand

Contents

Preface

about black men

---

don't believe the hype

When women get together and talk about men, the news is almost always bad news. If the topic gets specific and the focus is on black men the news is even worse. Despite all the advances in civil rights in our nation, feminist movement, sexual liberation, when the spotlight is on black males the message is usually that they have managed to stay stuck, that as a group they have not evolved with the times. Influential black male journalist Ellis Cose does little to dispel this image of black masculinity in his recent book *The Envy of the World: On Being a Black Man in America*. Yet his book has received more widespread attention than any other recent work focusing on black males.

Identifying black males as "a group apart" in the preface Cose contends:

Many of us are lost in this America of the twenty-first century. We are less sure of our place in the world than our predecessors, in part because our options, our potential choices, are so much grander than theirs. So we are trapped in a paradox. We know, whether we admit it openly or not, that in many respects things are better than they have ever been for us. This is a time, after all, when an African American [male] can be secretary of state and, possibly, even president. The old barriers that blocked us at every pass have finally fallen away—or they have opened up enough to allow a few of us to get through. But although it is fully within our power, collectively and individually, to achieve a level of success that would have been all but unimaginable for most of our forefathers, many of us are doomed to fail.

While Cose eloquently identifies many of the issues, he offers no vision of how black males might create new and different self-concepts.

The final chapter, titled "Twelve Things You Must Know to Survive and Thrive in America," offers his "new world rules," his keys to survival, or Cose's "commandments," or if you prefer "hard truths of this new age." His hard truths are at best simple commonsense advice about how to get along in the world and at worst trite platitudes. He encourages black men to stop complaining, stop blaming others for their plight, to ask for help, and to stay away from toxic associates. Hard Truth 11 states "even if you have to fake it, show some faith in yourself." Cose concludes his book with this disclaimer: "This volume is purposely less concerned with the systemic, with the grand social changes needed, than it is with the personal, with some things you might want to consider as you figure out how to live your life." *The Envy of the World* is a disappointing cultural analysis of the plight of black males precisely because Cose fails to link the personal, everything that is happening in the daily lives of black males, with the political, with progressive movements for social justice that offer theoretical and practical strategies that could be used to enhance the emotional well-being of black males and increase their chances of living fully and well.

Despite his direct appeal to black males in his last chapter, the language of Cose's book is that of the dispassionate observer. The book offers the kind of sketchy overview of black maleness that suggests its audiences are readers who simply do not have a clue about the experiences of black men. Even his chosen title, taken from the novel *Sula* by Toni Morrison, implies an audience of non-black males looking through the lens of their envy. Cose's book certainly lets them know that they have nothing to envy. In the novel a black woman is chastising a black male for suggesting that he is not getting enough attention. She says:

> I mean, I don't know what the fuss is about. I mean, everything in the world love you. White men love you. They spend so much time worrying about your penis they forget their own. . . . And white women? They chase you all to every corner of the earth, feel for you under every bed. . . . Colored women worry themselves into bad health just trying to hang on to your cuffs. Even little children, white and black, boys and girls—spend all their childhood eating their hearts out 'cause you don't love them. And if that ain't enough, you love yourselves. Nothing in the world loves a black man more than another black man. . . . It looks to me like you the envy of the world.

Though seductive in its use of the word *love*, close analysis shows that what is really being described is not love but desire. Perhaps what complaining black males want the world to hear is that envy and desire are not aspects of love.

Sadly, the real truth, which is a taboo to speak, is that this is a culture that does not love black males, that they are not loved by white men, white women, black women, or girls and boys. And that especially most black men do not love themselves. How could they, how could they be expected to love surrounded by so much envy, desire, hate? Black males in the culture of imperialist white-supremacist capitalist patriarchy are

feared but they are not loved. Of course part of the brainwash-
ing that takes place in a culture of domination is the confusion
of the two. Thriving on sadomasochist bonds, cultures of domination make desire for that which is despised take on the
appearance of care, of love. If black males were loved they
could hope for more than a life locked down, caged, confined;
they could imagine themselves beyond containment.

Whether in an actual prison or not, practically every black
male in the United States has been forced at some point in his
life to hold back the self he wants to express, to repress and
contain for fear of being attacked, slaughtered, destroyed.
Black males often exist in a prison of the mind unable to find
their way out. In patriarchal culture, all males learn a role that
restricts and confines. When race and class enter the picture,
along with patriarchy, then black males endure the worst impo-
sitions of gendered masculine patriarchal identity.

Seen as animals, brutes, natural born rapists, and murderers,
black men have had no real dramatic say when it comes to the way
they are represented. They have made few interventions on the
stereotype. As a consequence they are victimized by stereotypes
that were first articulated in the nineteenth century but hold sway
over the minds and imaginations of citizens of this nation in the
present day. Black males who refuse categorization are rare, for
the price of visibility in the contemporary world of white
supremacy is that black male identity be defined in relation to the
stereotype whether by embodying it or seeking to be other than
it. At the center of the way black male selfhood is constructed in
white-supremacist capitalist patriarchy is the image of the brute—
untamed, uncivilized, unthinking, and unfeeling.

Negative stereotypes about the nature of black masculinity
continue to overdetermine the identities black males are
allowed to fashion for themselves. The radical subculture of
black maleness that begin to emerge as a natural outcome of
militant anti-racist activism terrified racist white America. As
long as black males were deemed savages unable to rise above

their animal nature, they could be seen as a threat easily contained. It was the black male seeking liberation from the chains of imperialist white-supremacist capitalist patriarchy that had to be wiped out. This black man potential rebel, revolutionary, leader of the people could not be allowed to thrive.

More than any other black male who has come to power in our nation, Malcolm X embodied black male refusal to allow his identity to be defined by a system of race, gender, and class domination. His was the example that young black folks in the sixties followed as we struggled to educate ourselves for critical consciousness. We studied Malcolm's words, accepting that he gave us permission to liberate ourselves, to liberate the black male by any means necessary.

There is no mention of the legacy of Malcolm X in Ellis Cose's discussion of black male identity. The turbulent years of black power are remembered by Cose as marked by the murder of Fred Hampton. He recalls: "To me, the execution said volumes about the value of black male life in America, about how easily people could justify extinguishing it. But it also said a lot about fear; fear of the righteous anger of young, black men; fear of the potential power, bubbling beneath the system in the alienated hearts of the dispossessed." It fits with Cose's conservative narrative to forgo discussion of those individual black men who have courageously decolonized their minds and invented identities in resistance that transcend stereotypes. These black men, like W.E.B. DuBois and Malcolm X, did not see their success or failure in terms of wealth and fame. Their legacy has little meaning for masses of contempary black males because they struggled to challenge and change the system; they were not trying to make it work for them.

Wisely, individual radical black males understood and understand that imperialist white-supremacist capitalist patriarchy is an interrelated system of domination that will never fully empower black men. Right now that system is symbolically lynching masses of black men, choking off their very life, by making it all but impossible for them to learn basic reading and writing skills in childhood; by the promotion of addiction as the free enterprise system that works to provide unprecedented wealth to a few and short-term solace from collective pain for the many; by widespread unemployment; and the continued psychological lure of life-threatening patriarchal masculine behaviors. Anyone who claims to be concerned with the fate of black males in the United States who does not speak about the need for them to radicalize their consciousness to challenge patriarchy if they are to survive and flourish colludes with the existing system in keeping black men in their place, psychologically locked down, locked out.

Today it should be obvious to any thinker and writer speaking about black males that the primary genocidal threat, the force that endangers black male life, is patriarchal masculinity. For more than thirty years one aspect of my political activism has been working to educate a mass public about the impact of patriarchy and sexism in the lives of black folks. As an advocate of feminist politics, I have consistently called attention to the need for men to critique patriarchy and involve themselves in shaping feminist movement and addressing male liberation. In an essay written more than ten years ago titled "Reconstructing Black Masculinity," I suggest that "we can break the life threatening choke-hold patriarchal masculinity imposes on black men and create life sustaining visions of a reconstructed black masculinity that can provide black men ways to save their lies and the lives of their brothers and sisters in struggle." Yet despite this work and similar work by Michele Wallace, Gary Lemons, Essex Hemphill, and other advocates of feminist politics, our work has not influenced the more mainstream writing about black masculinity that continues to push the notion that all black men need to do to survive is to become better patriarchs.

Public refusal to face the reality that the plight of black males, young and old, is worsened by the collusion of all those who express concern, who even opportunistically rise to the occasion by shedding a spotlight on black masculinity, while refusing to tell the truth about what must happen to change this circumstance. Conservatives and radicals alike seem to be better at talking about the plight of the black male than they are at naming strategies of resistance that would offer hope and meaningful alternatives. Those of us, black women and men, who have consistently spoken about the need to educate for critical consciousness in diverse black communities about patriarchy and sexism rarely receive the attention of the mainstream when discussing the crisis of black masculinity. Our writing is not mentioned in conservative books on the subject.

However when I go to diverse black settings to teach and lecture, black males of all classes are in the audience. Listening to these men I hear and share their concern that black males are losing ground, that their plight is worsening. No matter how much we call attention to the crisis of black masculinity, there is yet no collective response. A feeling of despair threatens to snuff out our collective will to create positive intervention on behalf of black men. There is a general feeling of weariness that I see among my peers, a feeling that "black men just don't get it." Certainly the black males that I know most intimately don't seem to get it. At age eighty my father is still committed to patriarchal thought and action even though it keeps him isolated emotionally from loved ones, even though his sexism, and its concomitant violence and abuse, has ruined a marriage of more than fifty years. My brother who managed in his childhood to subvert patriarchal domination by remaining emotionally aware still strives to realize an unattainable ideal of patriarchal masculinity thus undermining the positive agency in his life. He often feels confused and discouraged. And the black males I have loved as partners have suffered the ravages of parental addiction and emotional neglect. Even though they are men who work hard, who are financially in good shape, they suffer emotionally.

All the black men that I love see themselves as isolated, cut off from any sense of group solidarity. They see most black male leaders as ineffectual hypocrites who are simply opportunists

looking out for number one. They share with Michele Wallace
the idea that: "When you look at so-called black leadership as
reflected by the mainstream media, what you see is a motley
crew of the narcissistic, the vaguely ridiculous, and the inept." I
tell audiences all the time who ask about the dearth of black leadership that there are radical visionaries among us willing and able
to lead us in the direction of liberation and the vast majority of
these folks are black women. Allegiance to sexist thinking about
the nature of leadership creates a blindspot that effectively prevents masses of black people from making use of theories and
practices of liberation when they are offered by women.

Realizing this I have hoped, along with radical black women
comrades, that individual black men who care about the plight
of black males and who are themselves advocates of feminist
thinking would do more work to reach out to black males as a
group. That work has not been forthcoming. Every time I
encounter a radical thinking brother I encourage him to write,
to share his wisdom with others. Many of the individual black
men working in the field of ending male violence against
women and children are experts at explaining black male crisis
and finding paths to healing, but they just feel they do not have
time to write. There is not even a small body of anti-patriarchal
literature speaking directly to black males about what they can
do to educate themselves for critical consciousness, guiding
them on the path of liberation.

The absence of this work stands as further testimony vali-
dating the contention that the plight of black men is not taken
seriously. An impressive body of literature arose in the wake of
black female resistance struggles aimed at challenging systems
of domination that were keeping us exploited and oppressed as
a group. That literature has helped black females to empower
ourselves. As both writer and reader of this work, I know that it
changes lives for the better.

I have often pondered why no body of resistance literature
has emerged from black males even though they actually own

magazines and publishing houses. They have control over mass media, however relative. The failure lies with the lack of collective radicalization on the part of black men (most powerful black men in media are conservatives who support patriarchal thinking). Individual charismatic black male leaders with a radical consciousness often become so enamored of their unique status as the black man who is different that they fail to share the good news with other black men. Or they allow themselves to be co-opted—seduced by the promise of greater monetary rewards and access to mainstream power that are the payoffs for pushing a less radical message.

As a black woman who cares about the plight of black men, I feel I can no longer wait for brothers to take the lead and spread the word. I have spent ten years waiting. And in those years the suffering of black men has intensified. Writing this book I hope to add my voice to the small chorus of voices speaking out on behalf of black male liberation. Black women cannot speak for black men. We can speak with them. And by so doing embody the practice of solidarity wherein dialogue is the foundation of true love.

I came to my love of black maleness from a childhood where the black man whose love I most craved regarded me with contempt. Luckily, Daddy Gus, my mother's father, gave me the love my heart longed for. Calm, tender, gentle, creative, a man of silence and peace, he offered me a vision of black masculinity that ran counter to the patriarchal norm. He was the first radical black man in my life. He laid the foundation. Always engaging me in dialogue, always supporting my longing for knowledge, and always encouraging me to speak my mind, I honor the covenant between us, the lessons of black male and female partnership grounded in mutuality he taught me by continuing to dialogue with black men, by continuing to do the work of true love.

Chapter 1

plantation patriarchy

Throughout our history in this nation African-Americans have had to search for images of our ancestors. When Ivan Van Sertima published his awesome work *They Came before Columbus* telling the world about the Africans who journeyed to this land before the colonizing Spaniards, it should have created an academic revolution, changing the nature of how American history is taught, particularly African-American history. Decolonized black folks realize that masses of African-American people once believed that ignorance was at the core of white anti-black racism. After a militant civil rights struggle led to new ways of knowing and those ways of knowing were systematically ignored by elites within the power structure, it became evident that the root of white supremacy was not ignorance but the desire on the part of unenlightened white people to maintain their dominance over black people in this nation and around the word. Even when liberal white individuals make popular movies, like *Amistad*, which offer radically dif-

ferent understanding of the role played by Africans in the so-
called new world, most citizens continue to believe that
African-American history begins with slavery.

African explorers coming to the "new world" before
Columbus were men. The fact that they did not seek to dominate and/or destroy the indigenous native people who were living on these shores reveals that their sense of masculinity was
not defined by the will to dominate and colonize folks who were
not like them. The fictive Africans in the film *Amistad* are sensitive spiritual learned men of feeling who struggle to cope with
the alien ways of colonizing white settlers. Compare and contrast this fictive image (a representation based on true
accounts) with the image of Africa, Africans, and African-
Americans interested in recognizing African roots in films like
Made in America and the more recent *Undercover Brother*. In
these films the black male who is interested in Africa is portrayed as a lying clownish buffoon, easily duped by faulty Afrocentric ideas. These negative images are created by white and
black males; they help maintain white-supremacist thinking.

Most black folks, particularly the black males who have power
within the mainstream film industry, focused their attention on
the flaws in the film *Amistad* basing their dislike on the fact that
it was created by whites. Very few viewers were willing to champion this film for the radical representation of black maleness
and Africa that was depicted. Yet this is the type of representation that should be seen by American moviegoers because it challenges stereotypes. Audience responses to this film expose a
great deal about the struggle for patriarchal power influential
black males engage in with white males, the unidentified gender
war that has been taking place since slavery ended.

When we read annals of history, the autobiographical writings of free and enslaved black men, it is revealed that initially
black males did not see themselves as sharing the same standpoint as white men about the nature of masculinity.
Transplanted African men, even those coming from communi-

ties where sex roles shaped the division of labor, where the status of men was different and most times higher than that of women, had to be taught to equate their higher status as men with the right to dominate women, they had to be taught patriarchal masculinity. They had to be taught that it was acceptable to use violence to establish patriarchal power. The gender politics of slavery and white-supremacist domination of free black men was the school where black men from different African tribes, with different languages and value systems, learned in the "new world," patriarchal masculinity.

Writing about the evolution of black male involvement in patriarchal masculinity in the essay "Reconstructing Black Masculinity" I write:

> Although the gendered politics of slavery denied black men the freedom to act as "men" within the definition set by white norms, this notion of manhood did become a standard used to measure black male progress. The narratives of Henry "Box" Brown, Josiah Henson, Frederick Douglass, and a host of other black men reveal that they saw "freedom" as that change in status that would enable them to fulfill the role of chivalric benevolent patriarch. Free, they would be men able to provide for and take care of their families. Describing how he wept as watched a white slave overseer beat his mother, William Wells Brown lamented, "Experience has taught me that nothing can be more heart-rending than for one to see a dear and beloved mother or sister tortured, and to hear their cries and not be able to render them assistance. But such is the position which an American slave occupies." Frederick Douglass did not feel his manhood affirmed by intellectual progress. It was affirmed when he fought man to man with the slave overseer. This struggle was a "turning point" in Douglass's life: "It rekindled in my breast the smoldering embers of liberty. It brought up my Baltimore dreams and revived a sense of my own manhood. I was a changed being after that fight. I was nothing before—I was a man now." The image of black masculinity that emerges from

slave narratives is one of hardworking men who longed to assume full patriarchal responsibility for families and kin.

This testimony shows that enslaved black males were socialized by white folks to believe that they should endeavor to become patriarchs by seeking to attain the freedom to provide and protect for black women, to be benevolent patriarchs. Benevolent patriarchs exercise their power without using force. And it was this notion of patriarchy that educated black men coming from slavery into freedom sought to mimic. However, a large majority of black men took as their standard the dominator model set by white masters. When slavery ended these black men often used violence to dominate black women, which was a repetition of the strategies of control white slavemasters used. Some newly freed black men would take their wives to the barn to beat them as the white owner had done. Clearly, by the time slavery ended patriarchal masculinity had become an accepted ideal for most black men, an ideal that would be reinforced by twentieth-century norms.

Despite the overwhelming support of patriarchal masculinity by black men, there was even in slavery those rare black males who repudiated the norms set by white oppressors. Individual black male renegades who either escaped from slavery or chose to change their circumstance once they were freed, often found refuge among Native Americans, thus moving into tribal cultures where patriarchal masculinity with its insistence on violence and subjugation of women and children was not the norm. Marriages between Native women and African-American men during reconstruction also created a context for different ways of being and living that were counter to the example of white Christian family life. In southern states enclaves of African folk who had escaped slavery or joined with renegade maroons once slavery ended kept alive African cultural retentions that also offered a subculture distinct from the culture imposed by whiteness.

With keen critical insight Rudolph Byrd, co-editor of the anthology *Traps: African American Men on Gender and Sexuality,* offers in his groundbreaking essay "The Tradition of John" the mythopoetic folk hero John as a figure of alternative masculinity. Byrd explains:

> Committed to the overthrow of slavery and the ideology of white supremacy, John is the supreme antagonist of "Old Massa" and the various hegemonic structures he and his descendants have created and, most disheartening, many of them predictably still cherish. In John's various acts of resistance are reflected his most exemplary values and attributes: motherwit, the power of laughter and song, self-assertion, self-examination, self-knowledge, a belief that life is process grounded in the fertile field of improvisation, hope, and most importantly, love. And his aspirations? Nothing less than the full and complete emancipation of Black people from every species of slavery. These are the constitutive elements and aspiration that together comprise the tradition of John. In these days of so many hours, it is a mode of Black masculinity grounded in enduring principles that possesses . . . a broad and vital instrumentality.

Clearly, the individual black males who strategized resistance to slavery, plotted paths to freedom, and who invented new lives for themselves and their people were working against the white-supremacist patriarchal norm. They were the men who set the stage for the black male abolitionists who supported more freedom for women. Alexander Crummell in his address before the Freedman's Aid Society in 1883 spoke directly to a program for racial uplift that would focus on black women, particularly on education. He announced in his address that: "The lot of the black man on the plantation has been sad and desolate enough; but the fate of the black woman has been awful! Her entire existence from the day she first landed, a naked victim of the slave-trade, has been degradation in its extremest forms."

Frederick Douglass spoke regularly on behalf of gender equality. In his 1888 talk "I Am a Radical Woman Suffrage Man" he made his position clear:

> The fundamental proposition of the woman suffrage movement is scarcely less simple than that of the anti-slavery movement. It assumes that woman is herself. That she belongs to herself, just as fully as man belongs to himself—that she is a person and has all the attributes of personality that can be claimed by man, and that her rights of person are equal in all respects to those of man. She has the same number of senses that distinguish man, and is like man a subject of human government, capable of understanding, obeying and being affected by law. That she is capable of forming an intelligent judgment as to the character of public men and public measures, and she may exercise her right of choice in respect both to the law and the lawmakers . . . nothing could be more simple or more reasonable.

Nineteenth-century black leaders were concerned about gender roles and exceptional black men supported gender equality. Martin Delaney stressed that both genders needed to work equally for racial uplift.

Like Frederick Douglass, Delaney felt that gender equality would strengthen the race, not that it would make black females independent and autonomous. As co-editors of the *North Star*, Douglass and Delaney had a masthead in 1847 which read "right is of no sex—truth is of no color." At the 1848 meeting of the National Negro Convention Delaney presented a proposal that began: "Whereas we fully believe in the equality of the sexes, therefore. . . ." Without a doubt black males have a historical legacy of pro-women's liberation to draw upon. Even so there were black male leaders who opposed Douglass's support of rights for women. In the essay "Reconstructing Black Masculinity" I state that most black men recognized the power-ful and necessary role black women had played as freedom fighters in the effort to abolish slavery, yet they still wanted black women to be subordinated. Explaining further:

> They wanted black women to conform to the gender norms set by white society. They wanted to be recognized as "men," as patriarchs, by other men, including white men. Yet they could not assume this position if black women were not willing to conform to prevailing sexist gender norms. Many black women who had endured white-supremacist patriarchal domination during slavery did not want to be dominated by black men after manumission. Like black men, they had contradictory positions on gender. On one hand they did not want to be "dominated," but on the other hand they wanted black men to be protectors and providers. After slavery ended, enormous tension and conflict emerged between black women and men as folks struggled to be self-determining. As they worked to create standards for community and family life, gender roles continued to be problematic.

These contradictions became the norm in black life.

In the early part of the twentieth century black male thinkers and leaders were, like their white male counterparts, debating the question of gender equality. Intellectual and activist W.E.B. DuBois writing on behalf of black women's rights in 1920 declared: "We cannot abolish the new economic freedom of women. We cannot imprison women again in a home or require them all on pain of death to be nurses and housekeepers. . . . The uplift of women is, next to the problem of the color and the peace movement, our greatest modern cause." Influenced by the work of black woman anti-sexist activist Anna Julia Cooper, DuBois never wavered in this belief that black women should be seen as co-equal with black men. Despite the stellar example of W.E.B. DuBois, who continually supported the rights of women overall, black males seemed to see the necessity of black females participating as co-equals in the struggle for racial uplift with the implicit understanding that once freedom was achieved black females would take their rightful place subordinate to the superior will of men. In keeping with sexist norms, sexist black folks believed that "slavery and racism sought the emasculation of Afro-American men" and that the responsibility of black folks to counter this, that black women were to "encourage and support the manhood of our men."

As editor of the "Women's Page" of the newspaper the *Negro World*, Amy Jacque Garvey, wife of the radical thinker Marcus Garvey, declared: "We are tired of hearing Negro men say, 'There is a better day coming' while they do nothing to usher in that day. We are becoming so impatient that we are getting in the front ranks and serve notice that we brush aside the halting, cowardly Negro leaders. . . . Mr. Black Man watch your step! . . . Strengthen your shaking knees and move forward, or we will displace you and lead on to victory and glory." This passage gives a good indication of the fact that educated black women struggled to repress their power to stand behind their men even as they were continually questioning this positionality. Outspoken women's rights advocates in the latter part of the nineteenth century, like Anna Julia Cooper, were more militant about the need for black women to have equal access to education and forms of power, especially economic power.

Throughout the 1900s black men and women debated the issues of gender equality. White-supremacist capitalist patriarchy's refusal to allow black males full access to employment while offering black females a place in the service economy created a context where black males and females could not conform to standard sexist roles in regard to work even if they wanted to. It was the participation of black women in the workforce that led to the notion that black women were "matriarchal leaders" in the home. In actuality, black female workers often handed their paychecks over to the males who occupied the patriarchal space of leadership in the home. Simply working did not mean black women were free. The gender roles that black folks formed in the twenties, thirties, and forties were complex.

It was not a simple world of black women working and there-fore exercising power in the home. Many contemporary black folks forget that in the world of the early twentieth century black people were far more likely to live with extended kin. A black woman who worked as a maid, a housekeeper, a laun-dress, etc., was far more likely to give her money toward the collective good and not for her own use or power.

While social critics looking at black life have continually emphasized the notion that black men were symbolically cas-trated because black women were often the primary breadwin-ners, they have called attention to the reality of the working black woman giving away her earnings. Not all black families cared about black women earning more as long as black males controlled their earnings. And now that a vast majority of white women in this nation work and many of them earn more than their white male spouses, the evidence is there to confirm that men are less concerned about who earns more and more con-cerned about who controls the money. If the man controls the money, even if his wife is wealthy, the evidence suggests that he will not feel emasculated. Black men and women have always had a diversity of gender roles, some black men wanting to be patriarchs and others turning away from the role. Long before contemporary feminist theory talked about the value of male participation in parenting, the idea that men could stay home and raise children while women worked had already been proven in black life.

Black women and men have never been praised for having created a diversity of gender roles. In the first essay I wrote about black masculinity more than ten years ago the lengthy arguments I made are worth quoting again here:

> Without implying that black women and men lived in gender utopia, I am suggesting that black sex roles, and particularly the role of men, have been more complex and problematized in black life than is believed. This was especially the case when all black

people lived in segregated neighborhoods. Racial integration has
had a profound impact on black gender roles. It has helped to promote a climate wherein most black women and men accept sexist
notions of gender roles. Unfortunately, many changes have
occurred in the way black people think about gender, yet the shift
from one standpoint to another has not been fully documented.
For example: To what extent did the civil rights movement, with its
definition of freedom as having equal opportunity with whites,
sanctioned looking at white gender roles as a norm black people
should imitate? Why has there been so little positive interest
shown in the alternative lifestyles of black men? In every segregated black community in the United States there are adult black
men married, unmarried, gay, straight, living in households where
they do not assert patriarchal domination and yet live fulfilled lives,
where they are not sitting around worried about castration. Again it
must be emphasized that the black men who are most worried
about castration and emasculation are those who have completely
absorbed white-supremacist patriarchal definitions of masculinity.

Black people begin to support patriarchy more as more civil
rights were gained and the contributions black women made to
the struggle for black liberation were no longer seen as essential and necessary contributions.

Significantly, when the white patriarchal world begins to turn
its critical gaze on black families, a negative critique of black
females becomes more commonplace. It had simply been an
accepted norm that given the politics of white supremacy and
racial injustice black women would struggle equally with black
men on all fronts to ensure racial uplift. At the very beginning of
the twentieth century the U.S. Census Bureau issued a warning
about the nature of black families, calling attention to the fact that
African-American women were disproportionately abandoned by
their husbands or had never married but had children. When E.
Franklin Frazier published his 1939 study *The Negro Family in the
United States* (which was considered groundbreaking at the time it

was written) he endeavored to call attention to the diversity of marital and partnership arrangements black people were making as well as the impact of class on black family relations. Frazier was one of the first academics to call attention to the way in which racist barriers to black people assuming sexist-defined roles disrupted marriage and black families because it led to a lack of interest in sustaining two-parent households. Yet Frazier never suggested that these arrangements were emasculating to black men.

Many males were as uninterested in traditional sexist roles as were females, if not more so. And unlike white males, black males did not have an institutionalized patriarchal-influenced morality to make them feel less manly if they abandoned families. In the fifties most black folks were trying to conform to patriarchal norms of marriage and family. Only 17 percent of black households were headed by women and homes with two parents present were more the accepted norm. Though limited, black females could find work in the service industry when there were no jobs available to black men, which meant that they were often primary breadwinners in black families.

There are no records to indicate whether masses of black men coming from a slave history where work was compulsory and oftentimes brutal saw work as crucial to their masculine identity. Educated black men, imitating the manners and mores of middle- and upper-class white men, were few in number, unlike their poorer illiterate black brothers, they were obsessed with the notion of protecting and providing for their families. Certainly, many black men adapted to the reality of white supremacy providing menial jobs for black women while denying employment to black men without either internalizing the blame for this situation or projecting it onto black women. Julius Lester wrote about this spirit of resistance to white norms in *Look Out, Whitey! Black Power's Gon' Get Your Mama*, explaining that: "It is partially true that blacks have accepted the white man's image of themselves. However, it is also true that they have resisted accepting this image. It is not an exaggeration to say that the history of blacks in

America is one of resistance. But that resistance has remained, for the most part, unorganized, and thus the difficulty in recognizing the struggle that has been constantly taking place. (The resistance in black people's lives has remained little known in America because the racism that exists in this country will not allow any other view of blacks to exist except the racist view. When other views are presented, racism prevents their acceptance, unless, of course, these other views are articulated by whites.)" It has served the interest of racism for white people to ignore positive aspects of black life, particularly any shift away from sexism. It was vital to white male self-esteem to belittle unconventional black masculinity, saying that these men were castrated.

When the United States government took a critical look at black families and Daniel Patrick Moynihan published his 1965 report, "The Negro Family," the imperialist white-supremacist capitalist state was the voice of authority positing the notion that black women had emasculated black males by being matriarchs and that participating in the armed forces by joining the military was one way for black men to reclaim their patriarchal status. The discourse of emasculation shifted from white supremacy and accountability for black male oppression to blaming black women. Sexist mores, which encouraged woman hating, influenced black men to place accountability onto black females for their woes. In reality even if every black woman had stopped working to stand by her man, racist discrimination and exploitation would still have made it impossible for black men to be patriarchs. Significantly, Moynihan's report came just in time to reinforce the notion that it was important for black males to fight in imperialist wars. Retrospectively, it is easy to see the reason the state helped stir up gender conflict between black women and men just as it was preparing to enter various wars around the world. Just before the United States declared war on Iraq in 2003, *Newsweek* magazine published a series of articles suggesting black women were emasculating black men by being dominant in the world of education and work.

Ironically, the imperialist white-supremacist capitalist state, which claimed the black family would be healthier if black men headed households, had no difficult taking men away from households and sending them far away from families to wage war, to sacrifice their lives for a country that was denying them full citizenship. The Moynihan report did not create gender warfare in black life; it simply validated the sexist beliefs of many African-American men and to a grave extent legitimized their efforts to subjugate black females. Just as unenlightened white men were attacking black families for not being headed by strong patriarchal men, white women (along with individual black females) spearheaded a women's liberation movement, which announced their refusal to remain subordinated, proclaiming their desire to be equal to the men of their class. Very little is written about the extent to which the image of emasculation that racist white males projected onto black males was indicative of the feelings of impotence many white men felt in their relationships with powerful white women. Even though Moynihan was suggesting black men were emasculated, in reality many black men were clearly stating that they would rather be playboys than providers any day. White men were attacking black men in the sixties for not fulfilling the patriarchal role when it came to work and family, and black men were telling white men that sexuality was the only real site where manhood mattered and there the black male ruled. On one hand some white males were accusing black men of being castrated and on the other hand other white males envied black males their refusal to wholeheartedly embrace the sexist norm.

Individual white males seeking alternatives to patriarchal masculinity turned to black men, especially artists and musicians, for new definitions of manhood. Writing about his fascination with black masculinity in the 1963 essay "My Negro Problem—And Ours," Norman Podhoretz declared: "Just as in childhood I envied Negroes for what seemed to me their superior masculinity, so I envy them today for what seems to be their superior physical grace and beauty." Black masculinity, then and now, was seen as the quintessential embodiment of man as "outsider" and "rebel." Black males had access to the "cool" white men longed for. Embracing this vision of black male cool in his 1960s essay "American Sexual Reference: Black Male" Amiri Baraka boldy stated that: "American white men are trained to be fags" and posed the question "Do you understand the softness of the white man, the weakness?" This attack on white masculinity, and others like it, were common among militant black power advocates. It was not a critique of patriarchy. It was a call to arms in which black men were asserting that white men did not fulfill the primal ideal of patriarchal manhood because they relied on technology to assert power rather than brute strength. And more importantly the sixties were the moment when black men declared that they were connected to white men, brothers under the skin, bound by masculinity, by a shared allegiance to patriarchy.

When black males began in the name of "black power" to completely embrace patriarchal masculinity, the historical movement for racial uplift rooted in nonviolence and gender equality was ruthlessly undermined. Whereas an unconventional perspective on masculinity had given black males alternative grounds on which to build healthy self-esteem, the embrace of patriarchal masculinity meant that most black men measuring against the norm would also be less than a man, failures, unable to realize the ideal. Such thinking led to grave psychological unrest and disease. Tragically, collectively black men began at this point in our nation's history to blame black women for their fate. This blaming ignited the flames of a gender war so intense that it has practically consumed the historical memory of black males and females working together equally for liberation, creating love in family and community. It has practically destroyed beyond recognition the representation of an alternative black man seeking freedom for self and loved ones, a rebel black man eager to create and make his own destiny. This is the image of the black male that must be recovered, restored, so that it can stand as the example of revolutionary manhood.

Chapter 2

gangsta culture

---

a piece of the action

Like their unenlightened white female counterparts who supported feminist movement until white males allowed them a
piece of the action, a cut of the monetary power pie, unenlightened black men supported black liberation until they were
offered their cut. After the slaughter of radical black men, the
emotional devastation of soul murder and actual murder, many
black people became cynical about freedom. They wanted
something more tangible, a goal that could be attained.
Historically, the goal black men had defined as needed for the
restoration of their patriarchal masculinity was equal pay for
equal work. Prior to the black power movement most black
men wanted jobs—equal pay for equal work—which was the
vision of basic civil rights. They wanted the economic power to
provide for themselves and family.

Black power militants were ruthless in their critique of capitalism. They unmasked the corruption in the labor force in
America announcing for the black man that whether or not he

15

had a legitimate job, one that would give him value in the eyes
of white folks, no longer mattered since nothing about the capitalist system was legitimate. Within that system everybody was
a thief, everybody a gangster, everybody on the take. This was
the struggle Lorraine Hansberry had prophetically predicted
would take place in her play *A Raisin in the Sun*. Critic
Margaret Wilkerson explains in her introduction to the collected last plays of Hansberry that a conflict about the type of
manhood black males would choose was waged in *A Raisin in
the Sun*. Rather than using the insurance money for better
housing and education, the play's protagonist Walter Lee, tired
of working as a chauffeur, wanted to make easy money by
investing in a liquor store.

Describing Walter Lee's internal struggle Wilkerson writes
that he "believes that the money itself is synonymous with life."
Indeed, when asked by his mother "since when did money
become life?" Walter Lee responds, "It was always life. . . . We
just did not know it." Learning to play the game from watching
white men, Walter believes in what Wilkerson calls a popular
notion of manhood that says "the possession of money and the
things it can buy will make him a man in the eyes of his family
and society." Torn between his father's legacy of benevolent
patriarchal masculinity and its concomitant work ethic and the
longing for power rooted in the will to dominate in conquer,
Lee, according to Wilkerson, is willing to "sacrifice his pride
and integrity for mercenary values." Walter Lee explains his
new generation's relationship to money: "There ain't no
causes—there ain't nothing but taking in this world, and he who
takes most is smartest—and it don't make a damn bit of difference how." Wilkerson sees the play as dramatizing a struggle
between "human values and integrity, which are forcing change
in a world where human worth is measured by the dollar." It is
the struggle between an older version of patriarchy and a new
version that is overly informed by the reality of advanced capitalism. In the old version, man as worker, as patriarchal head of

the household and provider, matters; in the new version, man as worker is a slave or cheap laborer. Even though he works he cannot make enough to head a household, and fundamentally as a worker he can be replaced. In the play *A Raisin in the Sun,* Walter Lee is able to resist the lure of hedonistic materialism. However by the late sixties and early seventies most black men had made the choice to identify their well-being, their manhood with making money by any means necessary.

Though fiercely anti-communist Martin Luther King, Jr. consistently warns black folks about the dangers of hedonistic materialism and consumerism. Warning his fellow citizens in the essay "Paul's Letter to American Christians" King states: "I understand that you have an economic system in America known as capitalism, through which you have accomplished wonders. You have become the richest nation in the world, and you have built the greatest system of production that history has every known. All of this is marvelous. But, Americans, there is the danger that you will misuse your capitalism. I still contend that the love of money is the root of much evil and may cause a man to become a gross materialist." King's prophetic warnings fell on deaf ears. The invitation to participate in competitive money-making capitalist work, when made by the imperialist white-supremacist capitalist patriarchal state, enticed masses of black folk, calling them away from the resistance struggle for liberation. Just as many white radicals came through the turbulent sixties and seventies only to find at the end of their journey that they were unable to truly give up access to money and power in the existing capitalist social structure (which they had critiqued as relentlessly as black militants had), black people were embracing capitalism wholeheartedly. The conservatization of sixties radicals began with their embracing an ethos of greed, one in which having enough money to be self-sufficient is not what matters, but having money to waste, having excess. Like their white counterparts, an ethos of greed began to permeate the psyches of black folks.

A significant number of black power militants, male and female, were among the first generation of black youth to be educated in predominantly white university settings. In those settings many of us learned for the first time that the values of honesty, integrity, and justice taught us by our parental care-givers in all black worlds were not the values that led to success in the world we had entered, the world of mainstream white culture. This is precisely the conflict Walter Lee has with his mother, Lena Younger, in *A Raisin in the Sun*. He tries to explain to her that the values she holds dear (being a person of integrity, being honest, sharing resources, placing humanist goals over material ones) are not the values that lead to eco-nomic success in a capitalist society. Facing these contradic-tions and the psychological disillusionment they created served as a catalyst for many black folks, newly educated in the white school, to first turn away from capitalism in disgust and then to turn toward it, eager to participate in a corrupt economy, will-ing to stand among those who exploit rather than with the exploited. An examination of the biography of individual black power–educated elites and/or organic intellectuals would reveal how many of them shifted their positions. They moved from brilliant critiques of white supremacy and capitalism into assimilating into whiteness and striving to get money by any means (selling dope, creating fashion, etc.).

Once money, and not the realization of a work ethic based on integrity and ethical values, became the sole measure of the man, more black men could enter the game. As long as the stakes were respectable jobs, work that would lead into the mainstream, black men did not stand a chance at beating the odds. When money became the goal, black men had a chance. In black communities hustling for money, even if that meant lying and cheating, became more acceptable if it brought home the bacon. A shift in class values occurs in black life when inte-gration comes and with it the idea that money is the primary marker of individual success, not how one acquires money.

Adopting that worldview changed the dynamics of work in black communities. Black men who could show they had money (no matter how they acquired it) could be among the powerful. It was this thinking that allowed hustlers in black communities to be seen as just as hardworking as their Wall Street counterparts. Writing about the practice of hustling in *Look Out, Whitey* Julius Lester explains:

> Today resistance manifests itself in what whites can only see as the "social ills" of the ghetto, i.e. crime, high school dropouts, unemployment, etc. In actuality, many blacks have consciously rebelled against the system and dropped out. After all, why waste your life working at a job you hate, getting paid next to nothing, when you make more money with half the effort. So, a new class is created, the hustler who gambles, runs numbers, pushes drugs, lives off women, and does anything to avoid going to "meet the man" five days a week, year in and year out. It is dangerous, rough, and a none too beautiful life, but it has some compensation: A modicum of self-respect and the respect of a good segment of the community is gained.

The developing of a vibrant yet deadly drug economy surfaced in black life and was accepted precisely because it was and is an outlaw job arena where money—big money—can be made.

Uniquely positioned to accept the devaluation of the work ethic, black males whose brute labor had helped build the foundation of advanced capitalism in this society had never been paid a living wage. Work had never been for them the site where their patriarchal manhood could be affirmed. My father was a fifties black male patriarch. He worked hard in his job as a custodian at the post office. He accepted without protest or complaint racial discrimination in wages (until the laws changed) and he accepted white folks treating him with disrespect daily. He provided for his family. Mama taught us to respect and admire this ability to provide, calling attention to the black families where there was no man providing. They, and black couples like them, Hansberry's hardworking parents for example, were the real-life prototypes on which the characterization of father and mother in *A Raisin in the Sun* were based. My father's father had been a sharecropper slaving in the white man's fields for low wages. My mother's father had done the occasional odd job, cleaning yards, selling fishing worms. In both cases their wives did service work to bring home income.

The patriarchs of my father's generation looked with contempt at the new generations of black males who were only concerned with making money. In his memoir, *Makes Me Wanna Holler: A Young Black Man in America*, Nathan McCall recalls in his chapter on "Work": "It seemed that my brothers and I viewed everything in life differently than our old man. We represented two generations of blacks that had come up in very distinct places and times. Coming from the Deep South, my stepfather believed that you had to ignore all the shit that white people dished out and learn to swallow pride for survival's sake. Cut from the civil rights mold, he believed blacks could overcome racism by slaving hard and making do with what little they had." Men, like my father, like McCall's stepdad, believe not just in working, they believe that there is more to life than making money. They believe that one can have a meaningful life even if you make low wages.

Both Martin Luther King, Jr. and Malcolm X were men who lived without excess money. Indeed, Malcolm X gave up a life of hustling where he had the money and the power to become a man of integrity. In *Look Out, Whitey*, Lester called attention to the fact that any hustler would give up his way of life "if he could find some other way of maintaining his dignity." Sadly, as the economy worsened and unemployment became a possibility in all classes, collectively black males did not gain greater access to better jobs and living wages. Demoralized black males who could not gain the types of employment that would affirm their patriarchal manhood could then feel more comfortable with a system that valued the acquisition of money as the standard of patriarchal male value. In some cases black males could have cash by taking money from wives and girlfriends, or by pimping women.

There has been very little research examining the attitudes toward work that have shaped the collective thinking of black males. More than any other group of men in this nation black males have realistically understood wage slavery. They have been far less likely than other groups of men to believe that employment will lead to self-esteem and self-respect. Black men are not counted among those groups of male workers Susan Faludi called attention to in *Stiffed: The Betrayal of the American Man* when she describes men coming to terms in the eighties and nineties for the first time with the fact that patriarchal masculinity was not being affirmed in the arena of work. Faludi laments that "there was something almost absurd about these men struggling, week after week, to recognize themselves as dominators when they were so clearly dominated." These men, almost all white, that Faludi describes are experiencing the disillusionment with the myth of work as access to patriarchal manhood that most black men have lived with from slavery to the present day. Faludi concludes her massive study by suggesting that disenfranchised male workers (again she focuses almost exclusively on white male workers) may be forced by circumstance to venture from the "conventional route" in order to find "a better way forward to a meaningful manhood." Had she seriously focused on black males as workers, Faludi would have found examples of unemployed men, of workers paid low wages for a lifetime of labor who have done just that—created meaningful alternatives.

Professional sports have constituted an alternative work arena for many black men. In that world the black male body once used and abused in a world of labor based on brute force could be transformed; elegance and grace could become the identifying signifiers of one's labor. Historically entering the world of professional sports was a profoundly political endeavor for black men. If you wanted to enter that world you had to be willing to push against racial boundaries and there was no real way to escape the political. From Joe Louis to Muhammad Ali, from Wilt Chamberlain to Kareem Abdul-Jabbar, professional sports was a location where many black males received their first education for critical consciousness about the politics of race and black male bodies. Playing professional sports was a primary work arena for black men to both assert patriarchal manhood or a humanist-based selfhood and make money. Today that arena has become so corrupted by the politics of materialist greed that it is rarely a location where an alternative masculinity rooted in dignity and selfhood can emerge. Yet it was there that gifted black male athletes, like Muhammad Ali, dared to forge alternative masculinities and assert a black male identity distinct from the stereotype. Writing about the world of boxing Eldridge Cleaver declared: "The boxing ring is the ultimate focus of masculinity in America, the two-fisted testing ground of manhood, and the heavy weight champion, as a symbol, is the real Mr. America." Ali refused to be on display as the ideal American primitive male; he mocked the patriarchal masculinity, exposing it as mere empty pose and posturing.

If patriarchal standards for manhood prized being silent and unemotional, Ali dared to speak out loudly, to be bold and boisterous, and express emotions, embodying joy, laughing, daring to be sad, to feel pain, and to express the hurt. Photographs capture Ali smiling, hugging black males, daring to be physically close. On my desk I have the image of Ali holding his mother, showing his love; everything a patriarchal man was not supposed to be and do. Ali let loose the boy within and swept us away with his laughter, his generosity of spirit, his heart. He expressed the playfulness macho men were supposed to repress and deny.

The unenlightened white world—which remains invested in perpetuating and maintaining racist stereotypes, albeit on a more sophisticated level than in the past—is far more pleased with a Muhammad Ali who has been reduced to brute strength without the sharp keen intelligence and critical wit that characterized his power as a politicized black athlete who dared to decolonize his mind. The Ali reduced to silent symbol of brute strength without an intelligent voice that speaks makes the money. In the minds of racist white folks Ali today is a symbol of the castrated black man, the eunuch who comes when his master calls. For this reason it is all the more vital that black folks and our allies in struggle keep alive the memory of Ali's words and vision as a champion of the human spirit working on behalf of the liberation of the exploited and oppressed. This is the powerful legacy Ali created, the alternative masculine identity.

When black males have not been able to achieve in the world of sports, they have looked to the world of music as a site of possibility, a location where alternative masculinity could be expressed. Certainly the musical culture of blues and jazz had its roots in the black male quest for a vocation that would require creativity and lend meaning to one's labor. In *Look Out, Whitey*, Lester explains: "The musician is another who lives a subterranean existence, playing at hole-in-the wall clubs or wherever he can get paid for playing. Often his impulse to be a musician is a strong distaste for the kind of work a black man is expected to do within the system. This is particularly true in the South, where many of the old time blues singers say frankly, 'I had to find a way to keep out of the cotton field, so I started picking the guitar.' To a black man, work means putting yourself directly under a white man on a job and having to do what he says. Refusal to do so means being fired. Thus, work becomes synonymous with loss of respect." While gifted individual black males have been and are exemplary in finding alternatives to patriarchal insistence that work for wages is the only respectful labor, many more black males have turned to cons and hustles as a way to make money.

In today's world, most upwardly mobile educated black males from privileged class backgrounds share with their poor and underclass counterparts an obsession with money as the marker of successful manhood. They are as easily corrupted as their disenfranchised brothers, if not more so because the monetary stakes, as well as the rewards in their mainstream work world, are higher. Making money is even more important to these men because they too, like black male workers before them, must still submit to the whims of whites. Assimilated black males who are "white identified" find it easier to submit to fickle arrogant white males (and white female bosses) in the work place. However, most black males suffer psychologically in the world of work whether they make loads of money or low wages from overt and covert racially based psychological terrorism. Integration has not intervened on the strategies of psychological terrorism that unenlightened white people use to maintain their dominance over black people.

Since the plantation does not exist anymore, the everyday work world becomes the location where that dominance can be enacted and reenacted again and again. In this way work in the United States continues to be stressful and more often than not demoralizing for most black males. Even a conservative, assimilated black male like Colin Powell, who has major access to money and power, suffers from the racialized disrespect shown him by his white male counterparts. He, as well as other powerful black men in a similar position, may consider that a small price to pay for being able to embrace fully patriarchal manhood and reap the full benefits. Most black men, who work in our nation, make low wages and do not receive rewards for enduring racialized humiliation in the workplace. They suffer this and must also cope with the demoralizing effects of not receiving a living wage.

This double jeopardy has been the breeding ground for profound cynicism about the nature of work. Nathan McCall writes about this in *Makes Me Wanna Holler* as he describes the demoralizing impact of racist aggression in his stepfather's work life: "In spite of his belief that work was the answer to overcoming racism, I could tell that race-related pressures at his full-time shipyard job were eating my stepfather up inside. He and co-workers who came to the house constantly complained about whites on the shipyard security force being promoted over more qualified blacks. . . . I never heard my friends say that they wanted to be like their fathers when they grew up. Why would we want that when we knew our father's were catching hell? . . . We didn't want to work for the white man and end up like him." This experience, witnessing a working black man stress out then later solace himself with alcohol, coupled with McCall's own negative experience made him contemptuous of work. By his late teens he was turned off by the whole idea of working in the system: "I took on the attitude about work that a lot of the brothers I knew had: 'If getting a job means I gotta work for the white man, then I don't want a motherfuckin' job." Bright young black men like McCall looked to the ideology of black power for their salvation. It was their place of solace.

Young beautiful brilliant black power male militants were the first black leftists to loudly call out the evils of capitalism. And during that call they unmasked wage slavery, naming it for what it was. Yet at the end of the day a black man needed money to live. If he was not going to get it working for the man, it could come from hustling his own people. Black power militants, having learned from Dr. King and Malcolm X how to call out the truth of capitalist-based materialism, identified it as gangsta culture. Patriarchal manhood was the theory and gangsta culture was its ultimate practice. No wonder then that black males of all ages living the protestant work ethic, submitting in the racist white world, envy the lowdown hustlers in the black communities who are not slaves to white power. As one young gang member put it, "working was considered weak."

Black men of all classes have come to see the market-driven capitalist society we are living in as a modern Babylon without rules, without any meaningful structure of law and order as a

world where "gangsta culture" is the norm. Powerful patriarchal players (mostly white but now and then men of color) in
mainstream corporate or high-paying government jobs do their
own version of the gangsta culture game; they just do not get
caught or when they do they know how to play so they do not
end up in jail for life or on death row. This is the big stage most
black male hustlers want to perform on, but they rarely get a
chance because they lack the educational preparation needed.
Or their lust for easy money that comes quick and fast does
them in: soul murder by greed. In his book *The Envy of the
World: On Being a Black Man in America*, Ellis Cose deliberately downplays the impact of racially based exploitation on
black men's lives. To make his point that black men, and not
systems of domination (which he suggests they should be able
to transcend with the right values), are the problem, he must
exclude any discussion of work, of joblessness.

Cose comes close to a discussion of work when he writes
about young black male investment in gangsta culture but he
never really highlights black male thinking about jobs and
careers. When discussing the lure of the "street" he makes the
important point that the street often seduces bright young
males attracting them to a life of hustling, of selling drugs. Cose
contends: "The lure of drug money for young inner-city boys is
so strong because it offers such huge rewards to those who otherwise would have very little." He quotes a former drug dealer
who puts it this way: "I came from poverty and I wanted nice
things and money and everything. . . . I quit high school and . . .
I just got caught up. . . . It was like, 'I'm eighteen. I want my
money now.'" The grandiose sense of entitlement to money that
this black male felt is part of the seduction package of patriarchal masculinity.

Every day black males face a culture that tells them that they
can never really achieve enough money or power to set them
free from racist white tyranny in the work world. Mass media
schools the young in the values of patriarchal masculinity. On

mass media screens today, whether television or movies, mainstream work is usually portrayed as irrelevant, money is god, and the outlaw guy who breaks the rules prevails. Contrary to the notion that black males are lured by the streets, mass media in patriarchal culture has already prepared them to seek themselves in the streets, to find their manhood in the streets, by the time they are six years old. Propaganda works best when the male mind is young and not yet schooled in the art of critical thinking. Few studies examine the link between black male fascination with gangsta culture and early childhood consumption of unchecked television and movies that glamorize brute patriarchal maleness. A biased imperialist white-supremacist patriarchal mass media teaches young black males that the street will be their only home. And it lets mainstream black males know that they are just an arrest away from being on the street. This media teaches young black males that the patriarchal man is a predator, that only the strong and the violent survive.

This is what the young black power males believed. It is why so many of them are dead. Gangsta culture is the essence of patriarchal masculinity. Popular culture tells young black males that only the predator will survive. Cleaver explains the message in *Soul on Ice*: "In a culture that secretly subscribes to the piratical ethic of 'every man for himself'—the social Darwinism of 'survival of the fittest' being far from dead, manifesting itself in our ratrace political system of competing parties, in our dog-eat-dog economic system of profit and loss, and in our adversary system of justice where truth is secondary to the skill and connections of the advocate—the logical culmination of this ethic, on a person-to-person level, is that the weak are seen as the natural and just prey of the strong." This is the ethic lots of boys in our society learn from mass media, but black boys, way too many of them fatherless, take it to heart.

Prisons in our nation are full of intelligent capable black men who could have accomplished their goals of making money in a responsible legitimate way but who commit crimes for small amounts of money because they cannot delay gratification. Locked down, utterly disenfranchised, black men in prison are in a place where critical reflection and education for critical consciousness could occur (as was the case for Malcolm X), but more often than not it is a place where patriarchal maleness is reinforced. Gangsta culture is even more glamorized in our nation's prisons because they are the modern jungle where only the strong survive. This is the epitome of the dog-eat-dog Darwinian universe Cleaver describes. Movies represent the caged black male as strong and powerful (this is the ultimate false consciousness) and yet these images are part of the propaganda that seduce and entice black male audiences of all classes. Black boys from privileged classes learn from this same media to envy the manhood of those who relish their roles as predators, who are eager to kill and be killed in their quest to get the money, to get on top.

In his memoir *The Ice Opinion*, rapper and actor Ice T talks about the lure of crime as a way to make easy money. Describing crime as "like any other job" he calls attention to the fact that most young black men have no problem with committing crimes if it gets them money. He makes the point that it is not only money that attracts black males to criminal activity, that "there's definitely something sexy about crime" because "it takes a lot of courage to fuck the system." There is rarely anything sexy about paid labor. Often black males choose crime to avoid the hierarchy in the workforce that places them on the bottom. As Ice T explains: "Crime is an equal-opportunity employer. It never discriminates. Anybody can enter the field. You don't need a college education. You don't need a G.E.D. You don't have to be any special color. You don't need white people to like you. You're self-employed. As a result, criminals are very independent people. They don't like to take orders. That's why they get into this business. There are no applications to fill out, no special dress codes. . . . There's a degree of freedom in being a criminal." Of course Ice T's cool description of crime seems rather pathetic when stacked against the large number of black males who are incarcerated, many of them for life, for "easy money" crimes that gained them less than a hundred dollars. The fantasy of easy money is pushed in popular culture by movies. It is pushed by state-supported lotteries. And part of the seduction is making individuals, especially men, feel that they deserve money they have not earned.

Of course there are lots of black males out in the world making money by legitimate and illegitimate means and they are still trapped in the pain of patriarchal masculinity. Unlike the world of responsible legitimate work, which, when not exploitative, can be humanizing, the world of money making, of greed, always dehumanizes. Hence the reality that black males who have "made it" in the mainstream often see their lives as empty and meaningless. They may be as nihilistic as their disenfranchised underclass poor black brothers. Both may turn to addiction as a way to ease the pain.

Very few black men of any class in this nation feel they are doing work they find meaningful, work that gives them a sense of purpose. Although there are more black male academics than ever before in our nation, even among the highest paid there is a lack of job satisfaction. Work satisfies black males more when it is not perceived to be the location of patriarchal manhood but rather when it is the site of meaningful social interaction as well as fulfilling labor. There has been a resurgence of black-owned businesses in the nineties precisely because many black male entrepreneurs find that racism abounds in work arenas to such a grave extent that even jobs they liked were still made unbearably stressful. Owning one's own business and being the boss has allowed individual black men to find dignity in labor.

Hedonistic materialist consumerism with its overemphasis on having money to waste has been a central cause of the demoralization among working men of all races. Responsible middle-class black men who embody all that is best about the

Protestant work ethic find that work satisfies best when it is not placed at the center of one's evaluation of manhood or selfhood but rather when it is seen simply as one aspect of a holistic life. At times an individual black male may be somewhat dissatisfied with his job and yet still feel it is worthwhile to endure this dissatisfaction because of the substantive ways he uses his wages to create a more meaningful life. This holds true for working black men across class. Throughout my life, I have been inspired by the example of my father. Working within a racist system where he was often treated disrespectfully by unenlightened white people, he still managed to have standards of excellence that governed his job performance. He, along with my mom, taught all his children the importance of commitment to work and giving your best at any job.

Despite these lessons our brother K. has been, throughout his life, lured by easy money. Lucky, in that his attempts to participate in gangsta culture happened early enough in his life to push him in other directions in midlife, he is still struggling to find a career path that will provide greater satisfaction for the soul. Like so many black males in our culture, he wants to make lots of money. Though he has a responsible well-paying job, his ability to be proud of where he is and what he has accomplished is often diminished by fantasies of having more. When he focuses his energies on doing more, rather than having more, his life satisfaction increases.

During the periods of his life when he was unemployed K. did spend his time working on self-development. Many black males in our culture face joblessness at some point in their lives. For some unemployment may be their lot for months, for others years. Patriarchal masculinity, which says that if a man is not a worker he is nothing, assaults the self-esteem of any man who absorbs this thinking. Often black males reject this way of thinking about work. This rejection is a positive gesture, but they often do not replace this rejection of the patriarchal norm with a constructive alternative.

Given the state of work in our nation, a future where wide-spread joblessness, downsizing, and reduction in wages is becoming more normal, all men, and black men in particular, are in need of alternative visions of work. Throughout their history in the United States decolonized black men have found those alternatives. Significantly, they see unemployment as time to nurture creativity and self-awareness. Not making money opened the space for them to rethink investment in materialism; it changed their perspectives. They engaged in a paradigm shift. Martin Luther King, Jr., in his critique of materialism, describes this shift as a "revolution of values." King invited black men and all men to "work within the framework of democracy to bring about a better distribution of wealth" using "powerful economic resources to eliminate poverty from the earth." Enlightened individual black men who make no money or not enough money have learned to turn away from the marketplace and turn toward being—finding out who they are, what they feel, and what they want out of life within and beyond the world of money. Even though they have not chosen "leisure" time, they have managed to use it productively. In his 1966 anti-war speech at Berkeley, Stokely Carmichael offered this utopian vision: "The society we seek to build among black people is not a capitalistic one. It is a society in which the spirit of community and of humanistic love prevail." Imagine the revolution of values and actions that would occur if black men were collectively committed to creating love and building community.

Until a progressive vision of productive unemployment can be shared with black men collectively, intervening on the patriarchal assumption that equates unemployment with loss of value as well as challenging the materialist assumption that you are what you can buy, most black men (like many of their white counterparts among the poor and disenfranchised) will continue to confront a work world and a culture of joblessness that demoralizes and dehumanizes the spirit. Black male material survival will be ensured only as they turn away from fantasies of wealth and the notion that money will solve all problems and make everything better, and turn toward the reality of sharing resources, reconceptualizing work, and using leisure for the practice of self-actualization.

Chapter 3

schooling black males

More than any other group of men in our society black males are perceived as lacking in intellectual skills. Stereotyped via racism and sexism as being more body than mind, black males are far more likely to be affirmed in imperialist white-supremacist capitalist patriarchy for appearing to be dumb or as we called it growing up in the fifties, appearing to be slow (meaning not quite bright). In childhood it was obvious to everyone in our all-black neighborhood that the thinking black man was perceived to be a threat by the racist world. There was no correlation made between one's ability to think, to process ideas, and level of schooling. Well-educated black men have learned to act as if they know nothing in a world where a smart black man risks punishment.

From slavery to the present day individual black men have been at the forefront of African-American efforts to acquire education on all levels. In the late nineteenth century and early part of the twentieth, any black male seeking to move from bondage to freedom looked to education as a way out. During this time a lack of material resources often led black families to send girl children to school and push boys to find work. In his 1930s autobiography *Black Boy* Richard Wright describes his shame about poverty and the resulting scarcity of clothing and books. "I began school at Howard Institute at a later age than was usual; my mother had not been able to buy me the necessary clothes to make me presentable." Like many black families suffering economic distress Wright's family was constantly moving, which meant his schooling was consistently interrupted: "Though I was nearly nine years of age, I had not had a single, unbroken year of school, and I was not conscious of it. I could read and count and that was about as much as most of the people I met could do, grown-ups or children." In a post-slavery Jim Crow world, black folks had to struggle for the right to educate themselves. And even when that right was gained, the immediate need for material survival often disrupted the efforts of black males to acquire education.

Nowadays in the imperialist white-supremacist capitalist patriarch culture, most boys from poor and underprivileged classes are socialized via mass media and class-biased education to believe that all that is required for their survival is the ability to do physical labor. Black boys, disproportionately numbered among the poor, have been socialized to believe that physical strength and stamina are all that really matter. That socialization is as much in place in today's world as it was during slavery. Groomed to remain permanent members of an underclass, groomed to be without choice and therefore ready to kill for the state in wars whenever needed, black males without class privilege have always been targeted for miseducation. They have been and are taught that "thinking" is not valuable labor, that "thinking" will not help them to survive. Tragically many black males have not resisted this socialization. It is no accident that many brilliant-thinking black males end up imprisoned for, even as boys, they were deemed threatening, bad, and dangerous.

During the grim periods of legally sanctioned racial segregation, discrimination, and oppression black males of all
classes were acutely aware of the need to resist these stereotypes. They were aware that embracing the stereotype could
be life-threatening. Biographies and autobiographies of black
men who managed to transcend the poverty they were born
into all tell stories of individuals who struggled to educate
themselves within educational systems that were not supportive. Richard Wright learned to read in early childhood and
enjoyed reading and thinking. Yet it put him at odds with a
racist white work world that just wanted a black man to be obedient and dumb. Wright recalls that reading books gave him a
vision of a different life, that by imagining himself as a writer
he "kept hope alive." Books taught him that there were different perspectives to have about life. Confessing that he wanted
his life to have meaning he writes: "I was building up in me a
dream which the entire educational system of the South had
been rigged to stifle. . . . I was beginning to dream the dreams
that the state had said were wrong." A reader and a thinker,
Wright was constantly interrogated by classmates and teachers
who wanted him to remain silent. They wanted to know "why
do you ask so many questions."

Wright is telling a true story of a young black male's
encounter with the public school system in the twenties, yet
black males of all ages tell the same stories today. Sharing memories of his school days, Ellis Cose writes about looking back
and realizing that poor black children "were deemed essentially
unteachable." Like Wright he recalls little affirmation of his
desire to learn: "That elementary school experience made it difficult for me to take school seriously. I was never a bad student,
but I simply didn't see it as a venue where much learning would
take place or where my mind would be stretched. And the more
schooling I received, the more my assessment was confirmed.
Like Wright, Cose was chastised for being a thinker, for asking
questions; "There was the teacher, in either third or fourth

grade, who told the class that Negroes had lazy tongues. It was her way, I think, of both challenging and reassuring us, of making us comfortable with our deficiencies in reading and pronunciation. . . . Then there was the seventh-grade teacher who chastised me when I questioned the level of the class reading material. Yes, she agreed, the books were written for fifth graders, but we were not capable of even fifth-grade work, so I had best shut my mouth and be grateful that the school had deigned to give us any books at all." Time and time again when telling their life stories black males describe being punished in schools for daring to think and question.

The curiosity that may be deemed a sign of genius in a white male child is viewed as trouble making when expressed by black boys. Writing about his childhood in the fifties, poet and educator Haki Madhubuti tells how his attitudes toward education were transformed by his reading of Richard Wright's story. He recalls: "At thirteen, my mother asked me to go to the Detroit Public Library to check out a book for her. The title of the book was *Black Boy* by Richard Wright. I refused to go because I didn't want to go anywhere asking for anything Black. The self-hatred that occupied my mind, body, and soul simply prohibited me. . . . I and millions of other young Blacks were products of a white educational system that at best taught us to read and respect the literary, creative, scientific, technological, and commercial development of others. No one actually told men 'you should hate yourself.' However, the images, symbols, products, creations, promotions, and authorities of white America all very subtly and often quite openly taught me white supremacy, taught me to hate myself." Reading *Black Boy* gave Madhubuti permission to learn, to be a critical thinker: "For the first time in my life I was reading words developed into ideas that were not insulting to my own personhood. . . . Upon completing *Black Boy* . . . I was somehow a different type of questioner in school and at home." Black male learners, like Madhubuti, often share the reality that unenlightened black teachers often stereotype black boys as much as non-black teachers do.

Writing about striving to get an education in the eighties in his autobiography *Makes Me Wanna Holler*, Nathan McCall describes the racial harassment he encountered as an eleven year old alone in a predominantly white school: "I was the only African American in most of my classes. When I walked into one room and sat down, the students near me would get up and move away. . . . It wasn't much better dealing with white teachers. They avoided eye contact with me as much as possible. . . . It was too much for an eleven-year-old to challenge, and I didn't try. Instead, I tried to become invisible. I kept to myself, remained quiet during class discussions, and never asked questions in or after class. I kept my eyes glued to my desk or looked straight ahead to avoid drawing attention to myself. I staggered, numb and withdrawn, through each school day." McCall's home was a two-parent household. His folks were not poor. They wanted him to excel in school and for a time he obliged. When McCall leaves the school as a teen to attend a school with more black students he chooses hanging out with the "cool" kids over studying: "After I started hanging, the purpose of school changed completely for me. It seemed more like a social arena than someplace to learn. The academic rigors lost their luster and the reward of making the honor role just wasn't the same. Suddenly, I didn't want to be seen carrying an armload of books, and I felt too self-conscious to join in class discussions." McCall saw his turning away from education as rejecting a world wherein he had been given the message he did not belong and would not belong no matter the degree of his intelligence.

In the autobiography *Finding Freedom: Writings from Death Row* Jarvis Jay Masters recalls holding the belief in early childhood that there was no way out of suffering. He arrived on death row with minimal reading and writing skills. The child of a violent addicted single mom he never considered education something that could change his fate. He believed he was doomed: "Looking back I realize it wasn't rage that motivated me, though I hid behind anger to avoid certain truths about my life. I remember once walking down the street, when I came across a tree growing in the pavement of a parking lot between cars. My first reaction was to look at it, study it, wonder. I thought, 'How is this possible?' But I wasn't in school, I'd never learn these things. I smashed the little tree because I knew I'd never go to school. There was no room for wonder in my life." Raised in foster care, as a young black teenager Masters saw himself as trapped. He despaired at an early age. Wright, who confronted a system of race and class oppression far more brutal than any Masters has known, had learned as a child how to beat the system. He read books that taught him how to hope. Masters regains his hope only in adulthood, on death row, where he has become educated, where books have helped him liberate his spirit.

Poignantly, Ellis Cose describes the way in which he learned to be "so mistrustful of school, so alienated from its methods, and so convinced that I was too smart to be there, that I was in no mood to give it my heart." In the essay "Fear and Doubt" Huey Newton writes about the ways poor black males long for education yet fear failing if they seek it: "They tell their children that things will be different for them if they are educated and skilled but there is absolutely nothing other than this occasional warning to stimulate education. Black people are great worshippers of education, even the lower socio-economic Black person, but at the same time they are afraid of having their fears verified." These feelings about early schooling are expressed by black males across class. In the memoir of my girlhood I write about attending all-black schools where black boys excelled and were deemed smarter than even the smartest girl and the way that changed when schools were integrated. White teachers were not eager to teach black boys and white parents were not eager to have black boys sitting next to their sons and daughters. Suddenly, smart black boys were invisible. When a "special" black boy was allowed to be in the gifted classes it was only after he had proven himself to be appropriately subordinate. Always, he was the lone smart boy who managed to excel, learned to be obedient, to keep his mouth shut. Smart black boys who wanted to be heard, then and now, often find themselves cast out, deemed troublemakers, and placed in slow classes or in special classes that are mere containment cells for those deemed delinquent. Individual poor and working-class boys who excel academically in the public school system without surrendering their spirit and integrity usually make it because they have an advocate, a parent, parental caregiver, or teacher who intervenes when the biased educational system threatens them with destruction.

One of the primary reasons black power advocates chose to work in schools administering breakfast and/or tutoring was the widespread recognition that educational systems were not only failing to educate the black poor but were content with this failure, content to blame the victim. Yet are six-, seven-, and eight-year-old black boys to blame because they cannot read or write? When slavery ended in 1865 and four million black folks were free, most of them could not read or write. According to the census of 1900, 57 percent of black males were illiterate. Now as we move onward in the twenty-first century, black males make up a huge percentage of those who are illiterate. Being unable to read and write or possessing rudimentary skill sets, poorly educated black males are unprepared to either enter the ranks of the unemployed or to stay there. Even before black boys encounter a genocidal street culture, they have been assaulted by the cultural genocide taking place in early childhood educational institutions where they are simply not taught.

Committed to creating books that represent young black males and place them at the center of universal stories, I wrote a children's book called *Be Boy Buzz*, which is a positive representation of the holistic selfhood of boys. The boys represented are black. The illustrator of the book is a white male. When the first illustrations were shown to me, I noticed that many of the images were of black boys in motion, running, jumping, playing; I requested images of black boys being still, enjoying solitude, reading. The image of a boy reading was particularly important to include because it is clear that this society sends black male children the message that they do not need to be readers. In some black families where reading is encouraged in girl children, a boy who likes to read is perceived as suspect, as on the road to being a "sissy." Certainly as long as black people buy into the notion of patriarchal manhood, which says that real men are all body and no mind, black boys who are cerebral, who want to read, and who love books will risk being ridiculed as not manly. Certainly television representations of the studious black male in comedic sitcoms (for example, Urkel on *Family Matters*) suggest that the studious black male is a freak, a monster. Parents allow black boys to consume this negative image then wonder why they do not want to be serious learners and engaged readers.

Reading has been a fundamental source of knowledge, power, and liberation for black males, especially many imprisoned adult black men. Concurrently, many unemployed responsible black men are illiterate and have no access to an educational structure that will teach them reading and writing. They may also be so consumed by feelings of shame that they did not master these skills in their youth that they refuse to seek education as adults. Adult black male prisoners, with time on their hands, more often than not relish the opportunity to learn reading and writing skills. Yet these were skills they should have learned in school early on in life.

Learning to read and write are basic skills that are needed if one is to work and be a fully productive citizen. These skills are not taught to most black males. Educational systems fail to impart or inspire learning in black males of all ages. Concurrently, many black males graduate from high schools reading and writing on a third- or fourth-grade level. The demands of work and family may lead them to stop reading and writing altogether, hence they lose the skills they once had rather than build upon them. I have taught many young black men in college classes, great readers and writers, who simply stop reading once they enter the work world. They say that they do not have time for reading. But they also say that reading feels stressful, especially if it makes them think about subjects that generate more feelings of powerlessness and hopelessness. They would rather have fun on their down time. Mostly they do not consider reading a pleasurable activity.

Unlike the men of my father's generation, who believed that they should be organic thinkers/intellectuals, today's black males focus on making money. When the men of my father's generation came home from menial low-paying jobs they wanted to engage in serious conversations. They read newspapers, books. And more often than not they did not let the white folks they worked for know that they were "thinkers." Again a distinction must be made between being educated and being a critical thinker, someone who reflects on the world.

Today many smart black men who have been well-educated know that they are not supposed to be critical thinkers and they do not try to be. A black man, even an educated one, who thinks critically is still regarded suspiciously in mainstream culture. Oftentimes educated black males in well-paying jobs learn to assume a "go along to get along" pose so as not to appear threatening to white co-workers. One single black male over age thirty working in a predominantly white female working environment found himself continually treated as a sex object. One young white female wrote him notes in her version of black English telling him that she was "willing to be his 'ho." Although aware of the racialized sexism in her gesture, he felt it would make it seem he was not a team player, not one of the group, if he was seen as unwilling to take this as a joke. Yet this middle-class black male who had never spoken broken English or a black patois was being forced to assume a "ghetto rap" that signified to his co-workers that he was really black.

While we often hear about privileged black men assuming a ghetto gangsta-boy style, we rarely hear about the pressure they get from white people to prove they are "really black." This pressure is part of the psychological racial arsenal for it constantly lets educated black people, especially black males, know that no amount of education will allow them to escape the imposition of racist stereotypes. Often in predominantly white educational settings, black males put on their ghetto minstrel show as a way of protecting themselves from white racialized rage. They want to appear harmless, not a threat, and to do so they have to entertain unenlightened folks by letting them know "I don't think I'm equal to you. I know my place. Even though I am educated I know you think I am still an animal at heart." In *Black Rage* psychiatrists William Grier and Price Cobbs describe what they call "a paradigmatic black man": This man is always described as "nice" by white people. In whatever integrated setting he works in, he is the standard against whom other blacks are measured. 'If they were all only like him, everything would be so much better.' He is passive, nonassertive, and nonaggressive. He has made a virtue of identification with the aggressor, and he has adopted an ingratiating and compliant manner." Biased racially integrated educational environments often require that black males meet these requirements in order to prove that they are teachable, that they can learn. In segregated educational structures it was simply an accepted reality that black males could and would excel academically. This is one of the reasons many black parents today support moves to create segregated schools. During the years of legalized racial segregation, no one in black communities saw education as a "white" thing.

During the post-1960s world of racial integration, educated black people often assimilated the logic of white supremacy lording it over black folks who they deemed inferior. These attitudes led many educationally disenfranchised black folks to begin to see the educated black person as an enemy. Anti-intellectualism abounds in the culture as a whole. Because of this, black folks, especially those who lived in a segregated world where access to education was not simple, who were not educated, were predisposed to be suspicious of educated black people. John McWhorter's right-wing polemic *Losing the Race: Self-Sabotage in Black America* makes the useful point that black people "have inherited anti-intellectualism from centuries of disenfranchisement" but falls short by not linking the anti-intellectualism of black folks to the overall anti-intellectualism in the culture. McWhorter has spent so much of his life among educated whites that he seems unable to face the anti-intellectualism that is taught by mass media, especially television. He insists that "anti-intellectualism is not foisted upon black Americans by whites, but passed on as a cultural trait." Of course to make this point McWhorter has to ignore the academic and intellectual legacy of African-Americans prior to the sixties.

Anti-intellectualism in black communities is often a weapon used in the class warfare between those black folks who feel condemned to a narrow existence because they are not educated and are therefore unable to be upwardly mobile and educated black folks who are striving to be among the professional managerial class. These privileged-class educated black folks have tended to regard the uneducated with contempt. And the uneducated have responded by reflecting that contempt. Yet we hear more about the latter than the former. Many of the young black power advocates were avid readers. They were well-educated critical thinkers. Some of them were organic intellectuals. There is no anti-intellectualism in their writing and no equation of education with being white. In the racially integrated world of schooling, black academics who have acquired an education as a means of social mobility often devalue their learning when conversing with uneducated blacks. Often times college-educated black folks feel alienated from black community. When given the opportunity to socialize and bond with black folks, they may belittle education as a way of connecting with an anti-intellectual black world. This is also a strategy of top ranking. They get to remain in their position as exceptional black elites by being gatekeepers who hoard the knowledge of the ways education empowers while pretending that it is meaningless.

Advocates of black self-determination have always prioritized education linking it with the development of critical consciousness and critical thinking. In fact black power advocates were more often than not critical of the existing educational system's miseducation of black folks and supported the formation of progressive black schools. In the early seventies Don L. Lee's book *From Plan to Planet: Life Studies—The Need for Afrikan Minds and Institutions* focused on the need for education. Urging black males to create progressive educational structures he writes: "Where are black men being trained? Mostly on the street corners or in the prisons. Why is it that our brothers do not develop a level of black consciousness on the outside that they develop inside? Why is it that most brothers gain their political awareness inside the prisons after 99 years to life has been slapped on them? Well, mainly because we have failed to build the necessary institutions to educate and redirect our men. . . . In our new wisdom it is fundamental that we begin to institutionalize our thoughts and actions and we need institutions for that." Don L. Lee (renamed Haki Madubuti) founded progressive schools.

In his early vision of institution building, a vision he shared with other anti-racist black males, he linked the creation of schools with black nationalism. Integration led many black people to forsake black nationalism because it was linked to racial separatism. Facing the failure of schooling to educate black males today, individuals, especially those who are Afrocentric, push for separate schools. Oftentimes separate schools for black boys are presented as the best educational alternative because of their emphasis on strict discipline instead of learning. Yet often it is not the strictness that leads boys to do well in these schools, rather the fact that they are cared about, given attention, and perceived to be learners who can excel academically. Individual boys educated in supportive environments often regress when they enter predominantly white schools where they are stereotypically categorized as non-learners.

Mass-based literacy programs, especially ones that would target unemployed black males, which link learning to the development of critical thinking, are needed to rectify the failure of early schooling. Home schooling as well as the formation of progressive private schools that educate for critical consciousness are important alternatives for black males. If black males can educate and/or reeducate themselves in prisons, it is all the more feasible that concerned black folks can school black male children rightly in the communities and homes where they live. In subcultures where such schooling is already taking place, black boys and black men reclaim their will to learn, to be educated despite the attempts by this society to crush the spirit and silence inquiring minds. Progressive schooling of black males can become a norm only as we begin to take their education seriously, restoring the link between learning and liberation.

Chapter 4

don't make me hurt you

---

black male violence

Read any article or book on black masculinity and it will convey the message that black men are violent. The authors may or may not agree that black male violence is justified, or a response to being victimized by racism but they do agree that black men as a group are out of control, wild, uncivilized, natural-born predators. Prior to the black power movement of the sixties, black men worked overtime to counter racist sexist stereotypes that represented them as beasts, monsters, demons. Indeed, many of the eighteenth- and nineteenth-century racist sexist stereotypes attributed to black males are traits that are today considered to be the mark of psychopaths. One of those traits was a lack of emotional responsiveness. It has been described as a missing conscience.

Therapist Donald Dutton, who has conducted research on violent men for more than twenty years, calls attention to studies that suggest that the brains of psychopaths do not work like

47

those of mentally stable individuals. Dutton explains: "The psychological syndrome of psychopathy includes the loss of the ability to imagine another person's fear or pain or the dreadful consequences that might follow abuse. Other key signs include shallow emotional responses and an unrealistic future scenario . . . accompanied by an unwillingness to examine past problems." Racist sexist iconography in Western culture during the eighteenth and nineteenth centuries depicted black males as uncivilized brutes without the capacity to feel complex emotions or the ability to experience either fear or remorse. According to racist ideology, white-supremacist subjugation of the black male was deemed necessary to contain the dehumanized beast. This perspective allowed racist folks to engage in extreme psychological denial when it came to assuming accountability for their ruthless and brutal dehumanization of black men.

Writing about this historical legacy in *Rituals of Blood* Orlando Patterson states: "In all these stereotypes we find the idea of the slave as a dishonorable brute whose maniacal desires must be kept in check by the master's discipline, and whose word can be accepted only under torture. . . . Seeing the victim as the aggressor and as the 'white man's burden' is a classic instance of projection: at once a denial of one's own moral perversity and violence and a perfect excuse for them. The demonization of the Afro-American male in American society is still very much with us." Yet what makes contemporary demonization of the black male different from that of the past is that many black males, no longer challenge this dehumanizing stereotype, instead they claim it as a mark of distinction, as the edge that they have over white males.

Black males who reject racist sexist stereotypes must still cope with the imposition onto them of qualities that have no relation to their lived experience. For example: a black male who is scrupulously honest may have to cope with co-workers treating him suspiciously because they see all black males as con artists in hiding. Nonviolent black males daily face a world that sees them as violent. Black men who are not sexual harassers or rapists confront a public that relates to them as though this is who they are underneath the skin. In actuality many black males explain their decision to become the "beast" as a surrender to realities they cannot change. And if you are going to be seen as a beast you may as well act like one. Young black males, particularly underclass males, often derive a sense of satisfaction from being able to create fear in others, particularly in white folks.

Yet fearful or not, it has really been mainstream white culture that both requires and rewards black men for acting like brutal psychopaths, that rewards them for their will to do horrific violence. Cultures of domination, like the United States, are founded on the principle that violence is necessary for the maintenance of the status quo. Orlando Patterson emphasizes that long before any young black male acts violent he is born into a culture that condones violence as a means of social control, that identifies patriarchal masculinity by the will to do violence. Showing aggression is the simplest way to assert patriarchal manhood. Men of all classes know this. As a consequence, all men living in a culture of violence must demonstrate at some point in their lives that they are capable of being violent. The movie *The Shawshank Redemption* is a prison story wherein the "soft" upper-class white man must prove he can survive in the predatory jungle of prison. His tutor is an older criminal black male. While the black male confesses to having murdered for no reason, the white male he tutors in the art of survival is shown to be innocent.

Another prison movie, *The Green Mile*, offers a similar image. The big "hypermasculine" black male who threatens to turn into a monster at any moment is shown becoming more and more civilized and domesticated as he develops the mysterious power to heal. His godlike power cannot, however, rescue him from being put to death for a crime he did not commit. In both these movies the "bad nigger" is alone and without any sheltering community—since in the John Wayne world of the west, real men go it alone. The frail sensitive white male Andy in *The Shawshank Redemption* proves his manliness by escaping from prison alone.

While the hypermasculine black male violent beast may have sprung from the pornographic imagination of racist whites, perversely militant anti-racist black power advocates felt that the black male would never be respected in this society if he did not cease subjugating himself to whiteness and show his willingness to kill. *Soledad Brother,* a collection of letters written by George Jackson during his prison stay, is full of his urging black males to show their allegiance to the struggle by their willingness to be violent. Paradoxically, by embracing the ethos of violence, Jackson and his militant comrades were not defying imperialist white-supremacist capitalist patriarchy; unwittingly, they were expressing their allegiance. By becoming violent they no longer have to feel themselves outside the cultural norms.

Violence is the norm in the United States. Orlando Patterson provides a background exposing the fascination with violence that is so pervasive in this nation:

> America has always been a violent place. And quite apart from their involvement with slavery, Euro-Americans have always exhibited a perverse fascination with violence. The violence of Euro-American men against other Euro-American men, and against Euro-American women, needs no documentation. The law of the jungle, of an eye for an eye, has played and continues to play, a central role in the culture. . . . Euro-American men exhibit a higher rate of homicide and other forms of violence than do the men of any other advanced industrial society. . . . America is the only advanced industrial society that practices capital punishment. . . . The experience, and fear, of violence among Euro-Americans is hardly new. . . . The quintessential

American myth is that of the cowboy. . . . Central to that myth
are the role of violence and the reverence for the gun. . . . Thus
violence is not only shunned and dreaded in American culture; it
is also embraced and romanticized.

Patterson makes the important point that most black males are
not criminals and calls attention to the reality that the typical
criminal is a Euro-American, explaining: "And if one includes
white-collar crime in one's count, as well as the unreported violence of . . . Euro-American males against their defenseless
wives and children . . . then it continues to be true that Euro-
American males commit not only the majority of crimes of violence in this country but the disproportionate number."
However, by projecting onto black males the trait of unchecked
primitive violence, white-supremacist culture makes it appear
that black men embody a brutal patriarchal maleness that white
men and women (and everyone else) must arm themselves to
repress. Sadly and strangely, individual black males have
allowed themselves to become poster boys of brute patriarchal
manhood and its concomitant woman-hating.

Retrospectively it is obvious that during the militant civil
rights movement the white-supremacist patriarchal states recognized that it would be a simple matter to encourage black
male fascination with violence. Although most folks remember
the Moynihan report suggesting black males were being symbolically castrated by black females, they often do not know
that his suggestion for how black men could restore their manhood was to send them to fight wars. White males acted as
though black male patriarchal behavior was acceptable because
black male bodies were needed to fight wars: both imperialist
wars abroad and gender war on the home front. Had the white-
supremacist patriarchal state wanted to, it could have imprisoned and slaughtered black males active in militant black
power movements for racial justice from the onset. It served
the interest of the state to socialize black males away from non-

violence (which was after all the powerful ethical position that had led many whites to join anti-racist civil rights struggle) and push them in the direction of violence.

Had white male leaders not condoned the violence of militant black males we would have no body of literature (published by mainstream presses) calling black men to armed struggle. Cleaver begin his *Soul on Ice* bragging about raping black women as practice for his rape of white women. He boasts: "I became a rapist. To refine my technique and modus operandi, I started out by practicing on black girls in the ghetto where dark and vicious deeds appear not as aberrations or deviations from the norm, but as part of the sufficiency of the Evil of a day—and when I considered myself smooth enough, I crossed the tracks and sought out white prey. I did this consciously, deliberately, willfully, methodically. . . . Rape was an insurrectionary act. It delighted men that I was defying and trampling upon the white man's laws, upon his system of values." This book was one of the first works published by a self-proclaimed revolutionary black man praising violence, sharing with the world that he had consciously chosen to become the brutal black beast of white racist imaginations. Powerful conservative, liberal, and radical white men were not afraid of the message Cleaver's work contained; they helped disseminate it. *Soul on Ice* sold millions of copies and has been recently reprinted. Cleaver's book received unprecedented acclaim for a nonfiction polemical book by a black male writer who expressed sexist, misogynist, and homophobic beliefs right at the historical moment when women's liberation and the movement for sexual liberation (with its focus on gay rights) were gaining momentum.

It is as though patriarchal white men decided that they could make use of militant black male sexism, letting it be the first and loudest voice of anti-feminist backlash. Polls and surveys of the population that looked at attitudes toward gender roles in the late sixties and early seventies actually showed that black males were much more supportive of women entering the workforce and receiving equal pay for equal work than other groups of men. The voice of black male sexism and misogyny was not representative. And yet it was that voice that received ongoing national attention. It was not the astute critiques of American foreign policy, of capitalism, that citizens of this nation heard from black power advocates. When they appeared in mass media it was only as agents proclaiming their right to do violence, their right to kill. This was one of the contradictions within black power rhetoric.

In *Look Out, Whitey! Black Power's Gon' Get Your Mama* Julius Lester critiques the violence of this nation, especially its oppression of black folks, then pages later encourages black folks to be violent. He writes: "America has the rhetoric of freedom and the reality of slavery. It talks of peace, while dropping bombs. It speaks of self-determination for all people, while moving to control the means of production on which self-determination depends . . . and if we seek to break out of this world, we're ostracized, clubbed, or murdered. Power maintains itself through rhetoric and force." Then he writes at the start of his last chapter: "It is clear that America as it now exists must be destroyed. There is no other way. It is impossible to live within this country and not become a thief or a murderer. Young blacks and young whites are beginning to say NO to thievery and murder. Black Power confronts White Power openly. . . . we will destroy you or die in the act of destroying." With radical political insight Stokely Carmichael said in an address at Berkeley, in October 1966: "I do not want to be a part of the American pie. The American pie means raping South Africa, beating Viet Nam, beating South America, raping the Philippines, raping every country you've been in. I don't want any of your blood money. I don't want it. We have grown up and we are the generation that has found this country to be a world power, that has found this country to be the wealthiest country in the world. We must question how she got her wealth. That's what we're questioning. And whether or not we want this country to continue being the wealthiest country in the world at the price of raping everybody across the world." Carmichael joined his black power colleagues in advocating violence, yet he always contextualized his support of violence making a distinction between revolutionary violence aimed at liberating the oppressed and the violence of oppressors. Yet these vital distinctions never reached a mass audience. What the masses heard was that black men were ready to kill.

Black males socialized in patriarchal culture to make manhood synonymous with domination and the control of others, with the use of violence, had believed during slavery, reconstruction, and the Jim Crow era they could not claim patriarchal manhood for fear of genocidal white patriarchal backlash. When powerful racist white men did not immediately crush militant black males who advocated violence, who acted violently, raping, killing, looting, it appeared that black males had finally arrived, their manhood was affirmed. Many of George Jackson's letters to his mother published in *Soledad Brother* express rage at her for domesticating him and his brother, for teaching them nonviolence, to be "good boys." He accuses her of repressing his manhood. Throughout all the published letters to family, friends, and colleagues Jackson shares his romanticization of violent resistance as the path to manhood. He shares his unquestioned belief in patriarchal ideals. Jackson entered prison at eighteen for a minor offense. After being accused of killing a prison guard he received a longer sentence. More than any other militant black male he epitomized black male youthful rebellion linked to a budding radical political consciousness. In *Soledad Brother*, with keen insight and sincerity, Jackson reveals the pain and crisis of a young black male's struggle to be self-determining, yet his assumption that patriarchal manhood expressed via violence is the answer is tragically naive. He wrote to his mother: "Being a woman you may expect to be and enjoy being tyrannized . . . but for me this is despicable. . . . You never wanted me to be a man. . . . You don't want us to resist and defend ourselves. What is wrong with you, Mama?" In other letters he tells her he is being a good boy. Jackson, like so many other black males, was seeking self-definition; he was unable to consider alternatives to patriarchal masculinity.

It would be all too easy to blame these black males for their uncritical embrace of patriarchy even as they were so critical of The Man, yet they were and remain, even in death, victims of sexist socialization. Had they been lucky they might have had individual black male renegades, true rebels against the patriarchal norm, to guide and mentor them. Were it not for their homophobia they might have found examples in the writing of gay black men. Experimental novelist, poet, and essayist Ishmael Reed writes in the introduction to the *Reed Reader* that he was inspired by the work of James Baldwin. Yet many of the black power males cite no elder black male they admire, who they want to be like. In the 1967 introduction to *Soul on Ice*, Maxwell Geismar says of Cleaver that his work reveals an "adolescent innocence—the innocence of genius." This spirit characterizes the confessional writing of many black militants. It is equally evident that there is an overwhelming degree of reactive rage expressed in these works that has the quality of a pathologically narcissistic adolescent whining because he cannot have everything he wants or what he wants is not just handed to him.

When Michele Wallace asserts in *Black Macho and the Myth of the Superwoman* that "the black revolutionary of the sixties calls to mind nothing so much as a child" she reenacts the same practice of psychological terrorism, the shaming and goading, that had been the breeding ground for unhealthy black male obsession with asserting manhood in the first place. However it is important to examine and name the connection between the sixties' militant black male embrace of patriarchal manhood and its concomitant violence and the more recent passive acceptance by too many black men of the notion that their manhood requires them to be predators, to be natural-born killers, or to symbolically represent themselves as such (i.e., rich rap artists who are in their lives nonviolent but who preach violence). Lots of young black men are walking around assuming a gangsta persona who have never and will never commit violent acts. Yet they collude with violent patriarchal culture by assuming this persona and perpetuating the negative racist/sexist stereotype that says "all black men are carriers of the violence we dread." Then there are the large numbers of underclass black males with no hope for the future who are actively violent. Added to this group are the black males who will never act violently outside the home, who do not commit crimes in the street, but who are, inside the home, in their private lives, abusive and violent. Overall the facts reveal that black males are more violent than ever before in this nation. And they are more likely to be violent toward another black person whom they deem less powerful.

Much black male violence is directed toward females. Sexism and the assumption of the male right to dominate serves as the catalyst for this violence. In the essay "Confessions of a Recovering Misogynist" Kevin Powell calls attention to the fact that black males in their twenties and early thirties who have been raised in the time of feminist movement and women's studies are as passionately misogynist and sexist as their older male counterparts. Writing about his violence toward women (as part of making amends) he confesses: "I, like most black men I know, have spent much of my life living in fear. Fear of white racism, fear of the circumstances that gave birth to me, fear of walking out my door wondering what humiliation will be mine today. Fear of black women—of their mouths, of their bodies, of their attitudes, of their hurts, of their fear of us black men. I felt fragile, as fragile as a bird with clipped wings, that day my ex-girlfriend stepped up her game and spoke back to men. Nothing in my world, nothing in my self-definition, prepared me for dealing with a woman as an equal. My world said women were inferior, that they must, at all costs, be put in their place, and my instant reaction was to do that." Black male violence against black females is the most acceptable form of acting out. Since the racist sexist white world sees black women as angry bitches who must be kept in check, it turns away from relational violence in black life. Mass media never cared or called attention to O.J. Simpson's violent abuse of black female partners, but when he was accused of murdering a white woman, the documentation was already in place to prove his violence toward her. Had the patriarchal state checked his violence when it was just a black-on-black thing, he might have learned nonviolence and never hurt another woman physically, including his white wife.

Black males today live in a world that pays them the most attention when they are violently acting out. Whether it is attention given to black men as perpetrators of violent crime (i.e., O.J. Simpson or the recent coverage in the mass media, particularly the *New York Times* of the "battle" between Harvard black professor Cornel West and the white male president of the university. (It is still a frightening commentary about the fascination this society has with violence that incredible amounts of money were made from mass media's exploitation of the brutal murder of Nicole Simpson via the invocation of the black male as murderous beast on the rampage.) In both cases symbolic shoot-outs occur in which black males are assigned the position of hypermasculine, out-of-control male body, and white males (whether enforcers of law or educators) are perceived to be acting with reason.

If black males are socialized from birth to embrace the notion that their manhood will be determined by whether or not they can dominate and control others and yet the political system they live within (imperialist white-supremacist capitalist patriarchy) prevents most of them from having access to socially acceptable positions of power and dominance, then they will claim their patriarchal manhood, through socially unacceptable channels. They will enact rituals of blood, of patriarchal manhood by using violence to dominate and control. Many black power activists started out as angry disappointed disenfranchised males who were unable to fulfill the patriarchal promise they had been told was their entitlement just for having been born male. They made themselves visible by unacceptable criminal behavior, by doing violent deeds. But when they were given the opportunity via legitimate socially acceptable civil rights struggle to bring positive purpose and meaning to their lives they sought to do so. And there was a difference between the violence they had enacted for criminal behavior and the violence they deployed in the interest of civil rights.

Ultimately they were, to use Lester's words, able to win and maintain power by using "rhetoric and force." Even though his critiques of the white patriarchal society were on target, he and his comrades were not able to offer alternatives to the existing structure or subversive ways to live within it. Lester writes: "White Power creates one basic condition under which all who are powerless must live: It makes us sharecroppers. We work at jobs we care nothing about so that we can buy food, pay the rent and buy clothes. We're paid enough so that we can stay alive and work and make money for somebody else. That's life in America." Without offering alternatives, his critiques, like those of his comrades, were not positive interventions. They laid the groundwork for the culture of cynicism that would become the norm once the movement ended; the nihilistic thinking that would be evoked to validate violence for the sake of violence.

After the black power militants lost their "armed" resistance struggle to the white male patriarchal state, they were left without a platform. Since their platforms (that is, the way they disseminated their message nationally) had been given them by the very imperialist capitalist patriarchal state they were claiming to want to overthrow, they were easy to silence. Mass media simply ignored any aspect of the black liberation struggle that was positive and ongoing. Their valuable messages of radical social critique, their call to end racist domination, and their demand for justice and freedom for all were soon forgotten by the masses. The images that everyone remembered were of beautiful black men wearing leather jackets and berets, armed with machine guns, poised and ready to strike. The message that lingered was that black men were able to do violence, that they had stood up to the white man, faced him down. No matter that they lost in the armed struggle; they had proven they were men by their willingness to die. And ultimately this is all that mattered. George Jackson made this position clear in a 1968 letter: "The symbol of the male here in North America has always been the gun, the knife, the club. Violence is extolled at every exchange: the TV, the motion pictures, the best selling books. The newspapers that sell best are those that carry the boldest, bloodiest, headlines the most sports coverage. To die for king and country is to die a hero." As dead patriarchal heroes black power militants have become icons, commodified celebrities, and yet their critical understanding of the nature of domination (including their vision of radical black nationalism) is not studied, enlarged, or treated as a starting point for new liberation struggle. Mostly it has been reduced to sentiment.

Theories of black superiority, of sun-people versus ice-people, replace the careful readings in historical materialism that were a norm as well as the vision of radical coalition politics (read all about it in the works of Huey P. Newton). Today's young and hip black male who fancies himself a radical, who is ready to throw down for the cause, is not talking about neocolonialism, about global struggle. And he is definitely not critiquing capitalism; making rap music is his way into the system. Radical activist and writer Kevin Powell puts it in perspective: "While I do not think hip-hop is any more sexist or misogynist than other forms of American culture, I do think it is the most explicit form of misogyny around today. . . . What folks don't understand is that hip-hop was created on the heels of civil rights era by impoverished black men and Latinos, who literally made something out of nothing. But in making that something out of nothing, many of us men of color have held tightly to white patriarchal notions of manhood—that is, the way to be a man is to have power. . . . Patriarchy, as manifest in hip-hop, is where we can have our version of power within this very oppressive society." Hip-hop is the place where young black males can deploy that rhetoric Julius Lester identified as a central aspect of power. Black male hip-hop artists who receive the most acclaim are busy pimping violence; peddling the racist/sexist stereotypes of the black male as primitive predator. Even though he may include radical rhetoric now and then, the hip-hop artist who wants to make "a killing" cannot afford to fully radicalize his consciousness. Hungry for power, he cannot guide himself or anyone else on the path to liberation. More often than not he is simply nostalgic about the past or seeking refuge in a fantasy of cultural separatism that is not functional in the work world today. But to not understand neo-colonialism is to not live fully in the present.

Perhaps that is the greatest tragedy of where we are as a nation in relation to black masculinity. Most black males are being encouraged through their uncritical acceptance of patriarchy to live in the past, to be stuck in time. More often than not they are stuck in the place of rage. And it is the breeding ground for the acts of violence large and small that ultimately do black men in. Black male violence is rarely, if ever rewarded—no matter what the patriarchal myth says. O.J. Simpson may walk the streets but he is a marked man; he is prey. And he has been preyed upon. It was a public feast, an old-fashioned lynching that had nothing to do with justice for Nicole Simpson or due process ("innocent until proven guilty") for O.J. Had the white patriarchal authorities cared about the life of Nicole Simpson they would have intervened during O.J.'s everyday violence.

White patriarchy is just as misogynist as black patriarchy and offers death as the price all women must pay if they get out of their place. Pretending to seek justice for Nicole Simpson, imperialist white-supremacist patriarchy simply cannibalized her mutilated dead body to feast on black male flesh. It was and is the new "birth of a nation." It was a full-fledged public announcement by a racist sexist legal system and mass media that black males, whether rich or poor, are still just demonic beasts in human flesh who must be hunted down and slaughtered. In *Native Son* Richard Wright described the black male confrontation with white patriarchy and the character of Bigger explained: "They choke you off the face of the earth. They don't even let you feel what you want to feel. They after you so hot and hard you can only feel what they doing to you. They kill you before you die." This nihilistic sentiment is the heart of the matter. Since so many black males, especially young black males, feel that they are living on borrowed time, just waiting to be locked down (imprisoned) or taken out (murdered), they may as well embrace their fate—kill and be killed.

These factors lead many black males to cultivate an abusive personality in childhood. It is a defense. Taught to believe the world is against them, that they are doomed to be victims; they assume the posture of victimizer. First embracing the ideals of patriarchal masculinity that make domination acceptable, they then draw upon misogyny and sexism to experience their first use of violence, psychological or physical, to control another human being. As we learn more about the life stories of black males active in the black power movement we hear tales of their abuse of women. Taught to believe that a real male is fearless, insensitive, egocentric, and invulnerable (all the traits powerful black men have in movies) a black man blocks out all emotions that interfere with this "cool" pose. Yet it is often in relationships with females, particular romantic bonds, that black males experience a disruption of the cool pose. They respond with anger and sexual predation to maintain their dominator stance. In his book on black masculinity Ellis Cose ponders why black males are more violent in romantic relationships without providing answers. He suggests that "most of the bad things many black men are accused of doing to black women they seem also to do to other women."

Misogynist rap music and the white male dominated patriarchal infrastructure that produces it encourages male contempt and disregard for females. It is the plantation economy, where black males labor in the field of gender and come out ready to defend their patriarchal manhood by all manner of violence against women and men whom they perceive to be weak and like women. Although it intensifies the problem of black male violence against women and children, misogynist rap did not create the problem. Patriarchy put in place the logic and patriarchal socialization that lets men take it to the level of practice. Hence the failure of men in power to intervene on O.J. Simpson's abuse of his wife.

Oftentimes the sexism in black communities, though intense, is so common that no one takes violence against females seriously. Violent actions by a black male may be explained as his response to racism and economic oppression (if that were the case black women would be gunning each other down and being equally violent to black males). In actuality there are powerful black males with "good" jobs who make lots of money who still act out violently toward women and children. Whatever the roots of black male rage, it is sexist thinking and practice that teaches them that it is acceptable to express that rage violently. Black male abuse of black females, both psychological and physical, is similarly present in black male relationships with each other. Black-on-black homicide is one of the leading causes of death in black life. It reminds us all that the violent black male has no real sense of agency, no real will to live. Analyzing black male violence from his experience, Ice T has come to understand violence this way: "Whenever somebody gets power, it's inevitable it will get abused. . . .

Frustration builds into aggressive behavior and it causes people to lash out and hurt somebody else. Anybody who suffers some kind of pain is searching to reach out. If you grow up in an aggressive environment, your threshold for pain grows higher and you're gonna do one of two things: You're gonna become extremely gentle or you're gonna become extremely violent." He sees the enraged black male as having a "mechanism in him he's trying to control" because he is "frustrated" he is "almost on the brink of insanity."

In imperialist white-supremacist capitalist patriarchy black males are socialized to be rage-oholics. As long as they are venting rage against other black people, no one really cares. Rage addiction will go unchecked until it becomes increasingly violent. This rage often has it roots in childhoods with no healthy caretaking, where abuse was the norm. Death row inmate Jarvis Jay Masters writes that he was taught in childhood to see violence as normal: "My stepfather tried to teach me how to hate as a child. He said it was for my own protection. He used to lock me between his legs and slap me on the head and face until rage filled my body. He'd say, 'Get mad . . . fight, son, fight,' and I would. Afterward, I'd be in pain, though more saddened for him. Once I contemplated stabbing him with a kitchen knife as he slept, but I couldn't do it." But clearly this indoctrination set Masters up for the violent actions that would take him into prison. Almost all violent black males have been abused as children. Yet they still believe that violence is an acceptable way to exert power, to influence a situation, to maintain control. Until there is a nationwide program against male violence that begins not with an examination of the violence men do to women and children, but with the violence men to do to themselves and other males, we will not end male violence.

As long as black males see no alternatives to patriarchal manhood they will nurture the beast within; they will be poised to strike. They will act on impulse, led by reactive rage. In the early nineties musician and critic Greg Tate, in the essay "Love and the Enemy," critiqued the limitations of any movement for black liberation based solely on rhetoric and a pretend display of force:

> When reaction rage is the dominant form of our politics, when it takes police or mob violence to galvanize us into reaction, it means that there is an acceptable level of suffering and misery. When quality of life issues are not given the same attention as our antilynching activities, it means we have a low level of life expectations. . . . The warriors we need to step forward now aren't the confrontational kind, but healers. Folk who know how to reach into where we really hurt, to the wounds we can't see and that nobody likes to talk about. If black male leadership doesn't move in the direction of recognizing the pain and trauma beneath the rage . . . if we don't exercise our power to love and heal each other by digging deep into our mutual woundedness, then what we're struggling for is merely the end of white supremacy—and not the salvaging of its victims.

Death by suicide, homicide, or soul murder is still just death, not the winning of a cause but a way to bow out. When black males are unable to move past reactive rage they get caught in the violence, colluding with their own psychic slaughter as well as with the very real deaths that occur when individuals see no alternatives.

Creative alternative ways to live, be, and act will come into being only when there is mass education for critical consciousness—an awakening to the awareness that collectively black male survival requires that they learn to challenge patriarchal notions of manhood, that they claim nonviolence as the only progressive stance to take in a world where all life is threatened by patriarchal imperialist war. If black males were to truly reclaim the legacy of Martin Luther King, Jr. and add to this political platform an awareness of the need to end male domination, they would be able to end the violence that is destroying black male life, minute by minute, day by day. It is no accident that just at the moment in our country's history when the nonviolent civil rights struggle rooted in a love ethic was successfully working to end discrimination, galvanizing the nation and the world—movements that included a critique of militarism, capitalism, and imperialism—the white-supremacist patriarchal state gave unprecedented positive attention to the black males who were advocating violence. It is no accident that just as Malcolm X was moving away from an anti-white black separatist discourse to global awareness of neo-colonialism, linking anti-racist struggle here at home with freedom struggles everywhere, his voice was silenced by state-supported black-on-black homicide.

The real agency and power of black liberation struggle was felt when black male leaders dared to turn away from primitive models of patriarchal violence and warfare toward a politics of cultural transformation rooted in love. These radical perspectives and the resistance struggle they put in place led to greater freedom. As powerful alternative visions, spearheaded by charismatic black male leaders who were not ashamed to admit mistakes, who were humble, who were willing to make sacrifices, they represented an absolute threat to the existing status quo. This is the masculinity black males must emulate if they are to survive whole.

To end black male violence black males must dare to embrace that revolution of values King writes about in *Where Do We Go from Here*: "The stability of the world house which is ours will involve a revolution of values to accompany the scientific and freedom revolution energizing the earth. We must rapidly begin the shift from a thing-oriented society to a person-oriented society. When machines and computers, profit motives and property rights are considered more important than people, the giant triplets of racism, materialism, and militarism are incapable of being conquered." Clearly, King's vision has proven to be far more radical than the political visions of black power advocates who embraced a militaristic vision of struggle. While King did not live long enough to undergo a conversion to feminist politics that would have enable him to critique his own negative actions toward women and change them, by insisting on the power of a love ethic he was offering a vision that, if realized, would challenge and change patriarchy.

Male violence is a central problem in our society. Black male violence simply mirrors the styles and habits of white male violence. It is not unique. What is unique to black male experience is the way in which acting violently often gets both attention and praise from the dominant culture. Even as it is being condemned black male violence is often deified. As Orlando Patterson suggests, as long as white males can deflect attention from their own brutal violence onto black males, black boys and men will receive contradictory messages about what is manly, about what is acceptable.

Contrary to the vision of black men who advocated black power, there is no freedom to be found in any dominator model of human relationships. As long as the will to dominate is there, the context for violence is there also. To end our cultural fascination with violence, and our imposition onto men in general and black men in particular who carry the weight of that violence, we must choose a partnership model that posits interbeing as the principle around which to organize family and community. And as Dr. King wisely understood, a love ethic should be the foundation. In love there is no will to violence.

Chapter 5

it's a dick thing

---

beyond sexual acting out

Undoubtedly, sexuality has been the site of many a black male's fall from grace. Irrespective of class, status, income, or level of education, for many black men sexuality remains the place where dysfunctional behavior first rears its ugly head. This is in part because of the convergence of racist sexist thinking about the black body, which has always projected onto the black body a hypersexuality. The history of the black male body begins in the United States with projections, with the imposition onto that body of white racist sexist pornographic sexual fantasies. Central to this fantasy is the idea of the black male rapist.

Until racial integration became an accepted norm, the fear of racial contact was always translated by racist white folks into a fear of black male sexuality. Euro-Americans seeking to leave behind a history of their brutal torture, rape, and enslavement of black bodies projected all their fears onto black bodies. If black women were raped in slavery it was because they were licentious and seductive, or so white men told themselves. If white men had an unusual obsession with black male genitalia it was because they had to understand the sexual primitive, the demonic beast in their midst. And if during lynchings they touched burnt flesh, exposed private parts, and cut off bits and pieces of black male bodies, white folks saw this ritualistic sacrifice as in no way a commentary on their obsession with black bodies, naked flesh, sexuality. (It is useful to remember the lynching of black folks escalated when slavery ended.) So much ritual sexualized torture of the black body indicates the intensity of both white hatred of black bodies and their longing to consume those bodies in a symbolic sexualized cannibalism.

Orlando Patterson's useful essay "Feast of Blood" explores this phenomenon. He explains that the body parts of lynched black folks were often photographed and the images sold. In some cases body parts were sold. Patterson writes: "If the victim was sometimes forced to cannibalize his own body, it was always the case that Euro-American lynchers cannibalized that of the victim." Most black men were lynched as retaliation for their assaults on white men. However, in the public imagination both in the past and in present, lynching is associated with sexuality. Patterson states that white folks desperately wanted to believe that lynchings of black males were a response to their violence and they "persisted in this belief even when confronted with the contradictory evidence of the lynchers themselves." Furthermore he explains: "The idea of Afro-American men resisting and fighting against the outrages heaped upon them was as much an anathema as was the fantasy of Afro-American men lusting after Euro-American women. Thus the distorting emphasis on the charge of rape and attempted rape accomplished two goals of 'racial' oppression in one fell swoop. It promoted the image of the Afro-American male as a sexual fiend, and at the same time it denied all manhood to him." This is the perverse historical backdrop that has shaped an informed black male sexuality, the ways black males see and feel about their bodies and the ways that they are seen and felt about by others.

There has been little or no speculation about the sexualities of African men prior to their life here in this country, either as immigrated free individuals or as enslaved captives. Yet one fact is more than evident: black male bodies were not coming to the new world obsessed with sexuality; they were coming from worlds where collective survival was more important than the acting out of sexual desire, and they were coming into a world where survival was more important than sexual desire. It is always difficult for Westerners to remember that places exist in the world where the ongoing obsession with sexuality that characterizes life in Europe and the Americas is simply not present. Since sexuality in the West has been linked to fantasies of domination from its inception (the domination of nature, of women) African people in the so-called new world were automatically entering a setting where the sexual script was encoded with sadomasochistic rituals of domination, of power and play. We know from slave narratives that black males and females found the white colonizers' obsession with sexuality strange. Naturally, they feared white sexual obsessions would lead them to be a target of sexualized racialized rage. For black women, being a target meant rape and mutilation; for black men, lynching and mutilation. No wonder then that in regards to sexuality Harriet Jacobs describes living in the home of racist white owners "a cage of obscene birds." Within this cage, black males working for freedom were eager to dissociate themselves from racialized sexual stereotypes. Even more than white puritanical slavers, they embraced the religious-based notion of the body and sexuality as sinful and endorsed Victorian notions of purity and sin. The end of slavery and abject subjugation in the immediate post-slavery years freed the black body from its containment within the scope of white racialized sexual fantasy. Living in a culture that eroticized domination and subordination, free

black males and females worked to construct habits of being
and lifestyles compatible with their unique experiences. The
formation of segregated communities, which removed the
black body from the white pornographic gaze, opened up a
space of sexual possibility.

Black males entered the twentieth century with very few
changes in their public status as subordinates in imperialist
white-supremacist capitalist patriarchy, yet the most radical
change happened in private, in the realm of the black body and
its sexual politics. For in the world of the home, a segregated
world away from the voyeuristic pornographic gaze of whiteness, black males and females had the freedom to explore their
sexuality, to reclaim and redefine it. Early in the twentieth century, black males and females sought to create an alternative
sexuality rooted in eros and sensual pleasure distinct from the
repressed sexuality of white racists and the puritanism that had
been embraced as a protective shield to ward off racist/sexist
stereotypes about black sexuality. Black males, deemed hypersexual in a negative way in the eyes of whites, were in the subculture of blackness deemed sexually healthy. The black male
body, deemed demonic in the eyes of white racist sexist stereotypes, was in the world of segregated black culture deemed
erotic, sensual, capable of giving and receiving pleasure.

Embracing patriarchal notions of manhood, black males
thought of sex as informed first and foremost by male desire. In
his essay "Patriarchal Sex" Robert Jensen explains: "Sex is fucking. In patriarchy, there is an imperative to fuck—in rape and
in 'normal' sex, with strangers and girlfriends and wives and
estranged wives and child. What matters in patriarchal sex is
the male need to fuck. When that need presents itself, sex
occurs." Much of the subculture of blackness in the early years
of the twentieth century was created in reaction and resistance
to the culture whites sought to impose on black folks. Since
whiteness had repressed black sexuality, in the subculture space
of blackness, sexual desire was expressed with degrees of aban-

don unheard of in white society. Unlike white women who turned away from heterosexual sex for fear of unwanted pregnancy, black women embraced the notion that it was a female's biological destiny to make babies. If sexual intercourse led to pregnancy, then one could not only accept this fate but rejoice in it.

Those black males who wanted to let the world know that they were engaged in the patriarchal sex that centralized fucking could do so by spreading their seed and making babies. In segregated black communities men in power (political leaders, the clergy, teachers) used their authority to sexually harass or seduce willing and unwilling females. Equating manhood with fucking, many black men saw status and economic success as synonymous with endless sexual conquest. Jensen writes that the "curriculum for sex education for a normal American boy" simply teaches males that they must "fuck women" or fuck somebody. Added to this lesson, Jensen says, was a notion that males should "fuck as many women as often as you can for as long as you can get away it" or "fuck a lot of women until you get tired of it, and then find one to marry and just fuck her." In segregated African-American life, patriarchal sex was not only the medium for the assertion of manhood; it was also reconceptualized in the space of blackness as entitled pleasure for black males who were not getting all the perks of patriarchal maleness in arenas where white men were still controlling the show.

Despite continued racial exploitation and oppression, when it came to sexual performance, black men in the segregated world of black sexuality could control everything and be the star of the show. In that world black males from any class, whether individually or in groups, could find affirmation of their power in sexual conquests. If, as Steve Bearman contends in his essay "Why Men Are So Obsessed with Sex," all males are offered sex as the location where they can experience "the great mystery of life," sex will be all the more valued by groups of men who feel their avenues for fulfillment are limited. On male sexual conditioning Bearman contends: "Directly and indirectly, we are handed sexuality as the one vehicle through which it might still be possible to express and experience the essential aspect of our humanness that has been slowly and systematically conditioned out of us. . . . That is why men are so obsessed with sex. We are born sensual creatures with an unlimited capacity to feel and an effortless propensity to deeply connect with all human beings. We are then subjected to continuous conditioning to repress sensuality, numb feelings, ignore our bodies, and separate from our natural closeness with our fellow human beings. All of these human needs are then promised to us by way of sex and sexuality." Of course sex can never fulfill all these needs, yet black men still seek it as though it can.

Like many males in patriarchal society, black male lust is fueled by sexual repression. In his essay "Fuel for Fantasy: The Ideological Construction of Male Lust" Michael Kimmel links sexual repression and sexism, calling attention to the way in which sexist assumptions lead men to contradictory notions about women's role in sexual desire. Kimmel writes, "Sexual repression produces a world in which the nonsexual is constantly eroticized—in fantasy, we re-create mentally what we have lost in real life." For many black males fantasy is not about what has been lost but what is seen as missing—as unattainable. And for many black males, what is missing is the potent sense of manhood they are told is the one form of power they can possess. If a black male does not possess this potency in real life then he can possess it via fantasy. Hence Kimmel's assertion that "sexual pleasure is rarely the goal in a sexual encounter; something far more important is on the line, our sense of ourselves as men." Men's sense of sexual scarcity and an almost compulsive need for sex to confirm manhood feed each other, creating a self-perpetuating cycle of sexual deprivation and despair."

In the iconography of black male sexuality, compulsive-obsessive fucking is represented as a form of power when in actuality it is an indication of extreme powerlessness. Though sexual myths project the image of the black male "pussy bandit," the "player" as the erotic hero leading this life of endless pleasure, behind the mask is the reality of suffering. "He can't get no satisfaction." This lack of satisfaction is the breeding ground for rage, and the rage the context for sexual violence. He can blame his inability to be satisfied on women. He can see females as the cause of his feelings of powerlessness. Kimmel suggests that most men do not feel powerful, that far from it, they "feel powerless and are often angry at women, whom they perceive as having sexual power over them: the power to arouse them and to give or withhold sex." These attitudes fuel "sexual fantasies and the desire for revenge." Individual black males have been more open about the rage and hatred they feel toward females, at times bragging about their sexual violence. This aspect of misogynist rap music is frightening. It reveals the extent to which patriarchal black males, like males in general, see sexuality as a war zone where they must assert dominance. If they cannot assert this dominance in real life, then it can be asserted in the realm of fantasy. Hence their desire for patriarchal pornography.

Precisely because black males have suffered and do suffer so much dehumanization in the context of imperialist white-supremacist capitalist patriarchy, they have brought to the realm of the sexual a level of compulsion that is oftentimes pathological. Bearman says that "sex quickly becomes addictive for most men." Sex has been all the more addictive for black males because sexuality is the primary place where they are told they will find fulfillment. No matter the daily assaults on their manhood that wound and cripple, the black male is encouraged to believe that sex and sexual healing will assuage his pain. Bearman writes:

> Sex, which will feel like the answer to your loneliness and deadness, will turn out to reinforce those feelings. You will come to

feel more alive when thinking about or engaged in sex than at almost any other time. When you do experience sex, you may come closer to another human being that you can remember ever being. . . . And so the closer you get, the more scared you will feel. And you will find ways to pull back, and you will begin to believe that is not safe and that you are just as alone as you have always felt. You will come to blame your partner or yourself for the inadequacy and for the inability of sex to make you back into the great, vulnerable, courageous, and free being you were born to be. But because some taste, some glimpse is available through sex, you will be driven to seek it out as the solution to your life-size dilemma.

This insightful analysis offers a useful paradigm for understanding black male compulsive sexuality. Sex becomes the ultimate playing field, where the quest for freedom can be pursued in a world that denies black males access to other forms of liberating power.

When the movement for sexual liberation intersected with racial integration in the sixties, for the first time black males were able to establish a public discourse about their sexuality. Yet what they revealed was first and foremost pornographic sexual obsession. Black male hustlers working as pimps bragged about being pussy gangstas reveling in their misogyny and woman-hating. Eldridge Cleaver's *Soul on Ice* was in part a sexual confession, revealing not only his need to control females' bodies but his obsession with fucking/raping white women as a way to get back at white men for oppressing him. Rather than repudiating the negative stereotypical image of the black male as a predatory and lust-filled rapist, Cleaver claimed this identity as central to his definition of black male being. Bragging about raping black females as preparation for raping white females, he states: "While I was defiling his women . . . I felt I was getting revenge." As the public discourse on black male sexuality flourished in the sixties and early seventies it became the site for black males to openly boast that they were more sexually competent than white males, that while white men might dominate them in other spheres of power, when it came to sexuality black men ruled. And the sex black males openly bragged about was centered always and only on conquest and penetration. In the chapter on sex in his memoir *The Ice Opinion*, Ice T shares his belief that sexual predation is normal in men: "Men are dogs. They would like to sniff it and fuck it, now if not sooner. . . . This instinct is simply in men. . . . The sex drive is so powerful that a man literally goes into this warp where he will do anything. . . . This is called hard dick insanity." Bearman contends that patriarchal sex insists on penetration. The foundation for this way of thinking about heterosexist intercourse is as Bearman describes "male-dominant—female-subordinate—copulation—whose—completion—and—purpose—is—the—male's—ejaculation." In patriarchal society much that is said about the heterosexual sexual predator is equally true for gay men since both groups are socialized to seek patriarchal sex. Through the dominant culture's fascination with the black male as a super sexual stud, they are able to mask their sense of powerlessness, their psychological sexual impotency, as well as their obsessive-compulsive dysfunctional sexual habits.

Deprived of a blueprint for healthy black male sexuality, most black males follow the racialized patriarchal script. The black males who collude in their sexual dehumanization often do so because they came into their own sexual awareness via sexual abuse, often at the hands of another black male. Black male therapist George Edmond Smith includes a chapter on sexual abuse in his book *Walking Proud: Black Men Living beyond the Stereotypes*. Unabashedly, Smith admits that "the frequency with which black men reveal to me that they were sexually abused as children astounds me." He contends: "Boys who are sexually abused or, for that matter, abused in any way are prone to negative behaviors as an adult and often become abusive to others." Melvin Van Peebles's 1971 film *Sweet*

Sweetback's Baadasssss Song graphically depicted the sexual abuse of a young black male by a grown woman. And even though the film depicts these sex scenes as "cool" the boy is portrayed as fearful. Yet the sex is offered as a rite of initiation ushering him into manhood. In his insightful book *Soul Babies: Black Popular Culture and the Post-Soul Aesthetic*, Mark Anthony Neal identifies the way black men are depicted in patriarchal pornographic imagination as embodying raw sex. He writes of *Sweet Sweetback*: "The dispassionate, workman-like nature of Sweetback's sexual activity is largely predicated on his role as a sex worker." Sweetback made his living and earned his initial notoriety performing in "sex plays" at a local whorehouse. He honed his skills with expert tutelage by the women in the brothel he is raised in. This connection is made very early in the film, when a young Sweetback, played by Van Peeble's pubescent son Mario, is subjected to a form of rape, which is portrayed in the film as a rite of passage.

Sexually abused by an adult woman prostitute, the young black male is overcome with fear. Not only does he fear that he will be unable to perform adequately, he fears that failure to service an adult woman sexually will mark him as unworthy to be a man. Neal explains: "This scene led Black Panther Party founder Huey Newton to suggest that the woman 'baptizes him [Sweetback] into his true manhood.' Like the sexual violence that Sweetback performs late in the film, Newton's logic speaks volumes about the subjugation of the weaker bodies of the black community, in this case children, to further the 'revolutionary' agendas of the ruling patriarchs."

Whether fucked by older females and males, or raped by male peers in childhood, the widespread sexual abuse of black boys receives little or no attention. The recent film *Antwone Fisher* based on a true story highlighted the traumatic sexual abuse of a little boy by a teenage girl. This was a rare depiction. Black boys are often encouraged to engage in intercourse with adults by grown men who think it is cool. Smith describes a client who had sex with an adult female when he was ten years old. The female, a prostitute, was provided by the boy's father as a birthday present. Smith writes: "In our group discussion, he reported the event as 'cool' in an attempt to impress others." Yet in actuality this experience of inappropriate sexual abuse had been traumatic: "The group member eventually shared with us how the prostitute had been aggressive with him and how he had felt inadequate during the whole encounter. As a young child, he had not been mature enough to handle the emotional impact of a sexual encounter. As an adult, he experiences a strong need to show women how adequately he performs sexually. In turn, he has been unable to sustain any long-term intimate relationship with a woman because of his need to constantly prove himself sexually." This is probably one of the common narratives of sexual abuse in black life, a boy forced to have sex with an older female against his will, because patriarchal thinking about sex suggests this is an acceptable rite of passage for a boy. When the sexual perpetrator is a male, the boy has no script of sexual coolness that would allow him to process openly this experience so he must internalize and hide his shame and his pain.

Black male public discourse about sexuality pointed the finger at white males and accused them of being pussies who were unable to get it up and keep it up. The black male who could not demolish white male power with weaponry was using his dick to "bitch slap" white men and by doing so sexually subjugating them. This sexual competition conducted via black male rhetoric created a window of opportunity for whites to openly revive their pornography obsession with the black male body without appearing to be racist. Certainly, white men were the group most fascinated and entertained by black male stories of sexual predation.

Much of the "hip" non-fiction literature by black males in the early seventies proclaiming their sexual prowess found a corresponding trend in "hip" white male non-fiction where the

expression of envy and desire of the black male body was commonplace. Expressing his fascination with black male cool,
white Beat poet Jack Kerouac declared: "The best the white
world offered was not enough, for me, not enough ecstasy, not
enough life, joy, kicks, darkness, music, not enough night."
Sexual liberation intersecting with civil rights and women's liberation opened the Pandora's box of racialized sexuality, revealing that little had changed. While white women could, in the
context of racial integration, make known their sexual desire for
black males and vice versa, more often than not that desire was
articulated and negotiated within the boundaries of racist sexist
archetypes. Embedded in much of the literature about black
self-determination and black power published in the sixties and
seventies was a subtext about black male sexuality. It silences
overt discourses of healthy black sexuality. The constant graphic
representation of black manhood as castrated and emasculated
became the victimology script many black males deployed to
deflect attention and criticism away from the compulsive-
obsessive nature of their sexuality as well as the justification for
sexual acting out. Despite the power of white male patriarchy it
is difficult to imagine that any white male would have been celebrated in the late sixties (at the height of the movement for
women's liberation) for being a rapist. And yet black males,
courtesy of Eldridge Cleaver and others, were stoking the fires
of white racialized sexist pornographic fantasies by proclaiming
that they were indeed the sexual fiends white folks had always
claimed them to be.

By the end of the seventies the feared yet desired black
male body had become as objectified as it was during slavery,
only a seemingly positive twist had been added to the racist sexist objectification: the black male body had become the site for
the personification of everyone's desire. In the contemporary
social context of hedonistic sexual desire where fantasies of
domination and submission are represented as "cool," the actual
lynching, castration, and cannibalization of the black male body

is replaced by symbolic slaughter and consumption. The dreadful black male body is transfigured into the desired body. This shift created an equal opportunity for all on the sexual terrain. As Cornel West explains in his essay "On Black Sexuality" the "subterranean cultural current of interracial interaction increased" and opened a space where there was "white access to black bodies on an equal basis." But as West points out, this shift takes place in a context where there is yet no demythologizing of black sexuality. Whites seek the black body to confirm that it is the exotic supersexed flesh of their fantasies. Within this economy of desire, which is anything but equal, the "hypermasculine black male sexuality" is feminized and tamed by a process of commodification that denies its agency and makes it serve the desires of others, especially white sexual lust. In *Rituals of Blood* Orlando Patterson writes: "It is no longer necessary for the image of the Afro-American male body to be used indirectly by Euro-American performers masking themselves in it. The Afro-American male body—as superathlete, as irresistible entertainer, as fashionable counterculture activists, as sexual outlaw, as gangster, as 'cool pose' rapper, as homeboy fashion icon—is now directly accessible as the nation's Dionysian representation, the man-child of Zeus, playing himself, wearing the ultimate mask, which is the likeness of himself." This is the only path to visibility black males are given permission to follow in imperialist white-supremacist capitalist patriarchy.

In "On Black Sexuality" Cornel West suggests that "white fear of black sexuality is a basic ingredient of white racism." However, the contemporary cannibalization of sexualized black male bodies in mainstream popular control suggests that white folks have found a way to conquer their fear. In the essay "Feminism Inside: Toward a Black Body Politic" I write: "Within neo-colonial white-supremacist capitalist patriarchy, the black male body continues to be perceived as the embodiment of bestial, violent, penis-as-weapon hypermasculine assertion. Psychohistories of white racism have always called attention to the tension between the construction of the black male body as danger and the underlying eroticization that always then imagines that body as a location for trangressive pleasure. It has taken contemporary commodification of the blackness to teach the world that this perceived threat, whether real or symbolic, can be diffused by a process of fetishization that renders the black masculine 'menace' feminine through a process of patriarchal objectification." At a time when black males are losing ground on all fronts, and in many cases losing their lives, rather than creating a politics of resistance, many black males are simply acquiescing, playing the role of sexual minstrel. Exploiting mainstream racialized sexist stereotypes they go along to get along, feeling no rage that they must play the part of rapist or hypersexual stud to gain visibility.

Many womanizing black males have experienced traumatic sexual abuse in childhood. It scars them for life. And when they receive the message from the culture that real men should be able to endure abuse as a rite of passage and emerge with their sexual agency intact, there is no cultural space for them to articulate that they were sexually abused, that they are damaged and in need of sexual healing. Therapist John Bradshaw identifies emotional abuse as the most common form of child abuse, which in many cases lays the foundation for physical and sexual abuse. He contends that "emotional abuse includes the shaming of all emotions, name calling and labeling, judgements, and sadistic teaching." In black family life these practices often come under the rubric of "signifying" and a child who responds to them by expressing pain (especially a male child) is just forced to endure more shaming.

Because individual adult black males (particulary academics) have interpreted signifying as a positive aspect of black culture it has been practically impossible to discuss the traumatic effects it has had on black male selfhood. Since much signifying centers on the sexual, it is often the emotionally abusive context in which black boys are traumatically wounded. They cannot express their pain because they are told that they must endure these rites of initiation to become "men." It is this early foundation of emotional abuse around the issue of sexuality that prepares black boys for later sexual victimization and/or physical abuse. Physical abuse creates body shame. Bradshaw explains: "When we are hit, and hit often and without warning, our body boundary is violated. We feel like we have no protection. The message we get is that any adult has the right to touch us or hit us or humiliate us." Broadening the definition of sexual abuse Bradshaw suggests that it can take these forms: physical sexual abuse, overt sexual abuse (voyeurism, exhibitionism), or covert sexual abuse (usually through sexual talking, like a grown man calling women whores or cunts). The last usually involves not receiving adequate sexual information and boundary violation (i.e., witnessing adult sexual behavior) and emotional sexual abuse. Lots of young black males engage in early sexual behavior with same-age children. Bradshaw says this is not necessarily sexually abusive: "The rule of thumb is that when a child is experiencing sexual 'acting out' at the hands of a child three or four years older, it is sexually abusive." Because this society has deemed black males hypersexual, the sexual abuse of black boys is simply not acknowledged. Or when it is acknowledged the presumption is that it has not been traumatic. Like therapist George Smith, in my interviews and conversations with black males I hear many stories of sexual abuse. And as Bradshaw emphasizes in *Healing the Shame That Binds You*, the sexually abused child often becomes a sexual addict, reenacting sexual or physical violation.

The backdrop of sexual abuse in black male life explains why it has been difficult for some black males to resist sexual objectification, sexual addiction, and the imposition of negative stereotypes. While popular culture more often than not calls attention to the supersexuality of black male hustlers, entertainers, and sports figures, little attention is given to the black male with status and class privilege who risks all that he has worked hard to attain by sexual acting out. This is evident in university settings when professors use their power to prey on students. It is evident in religious circles where clergy prey on parishioners (for example, Martin Luther King Jr.'s compulsive sexual behavior). And in everyday life where hard-working, clean-living black males act out sexually, compulsively revealing Dr. Jekyll/Mr. Hyde personalities that give new meaning to terms like *multiple personality* and *dissociative identity disorder*. It all gets just swept under the "black boys will be black boys" (i.e., sexual fiends and predators) rug. Concretely, this widespread denial helps maintain black sexual dysfunction. If the problem cannot be fully and adequately named, it cannot be addressed.

In imperialist white-supremacist capitalist patriarchal culture, hatred of black masculinity finds its most intense expression in the realm of the sexual. The dehumanization of the black male sexual body (often taking place with black male consent) is widespread and normalized. There are few places black males can go to get the sexual healing they need that would allow them to exert healthy sexual agency. Victimized by racist white projections of sexual pathology, most black males fear that naming dysfunctional sexual behavior is tantamount to agreeing that the black male is pathological. This is the type of identity forged in reaction that keeps black males from inventing liberatory selfhood.

Black men can claim the space of healthy sexual agency by moving from reaction to resistance. In an interview about black male lust, "When I Get That Feeling," Cleo Manago resists by refusing to allow the white interviewer to suggest there are perks black males receive in exchange for their submitting to objectification and sexual dehumanization. Asserting the power of his agency Manago responds: "Sometimes, to survive, we attempt to take advantage of expectations or assumptions of high sexual capacity, for example, but ultimately this feels contrived, dissociative, and dehumanizing, Not being seen fully and accepted as such can be very heartbreaking. Where's the perk in that? I think that perk thing is a bizarre romantic assumption made by some Whites. There are not healthy benefits to being Black, sexy, or more beautiful in a society run by Whites who resent and feel challenged by your beauty, who are obsessed with controlling or dominating you in reaction to the self-consciousness they feel in your presence. . . . This is a precarious place to be. I don't agree that Black men are more embodied than white men." Indeed, perhaps this is the starting place for collective black male sexual healing: the refusal to lay claim to a pleasure in the body that is just not true to the lived experience of most black men. Perhaps the formation of therapeutic sites for sexual healing will allow black men to speak a sexual longing that is not informed by sexual violence, either the racialized sexual violence imposed by whiteness or the hypermasculine mask imposed by blackness.

To claim the space of healthy erotic agency black males (and those of us who truly love the black male body) must envision together a new kind of sex, a non-patriarchal sexual identity. We must envision a liberatory sexuality that refuses to ground sexual acts in narratives of domination and submission, and lay claim to uninhibited erotic agency that prioritizes connection and mutuality. Enlightened anti-patriarchal males are creating new sexual maps. Steve Bearman urges men to find their way to genuine sexual agency by reclaiming the body, feelings, intimacy. Rightly he contends: "When sexual desire is purged of desperation, urgency, loneliness, and fear, then sex can be inspired by joy and sexual relationships can be healthy and whole." Black males are in need of sexual healing. Such healing happens every time we create the culture of resistance where black male bodies and being are no longer held captive. A free black man, at home in his body, able to feel his sexual desire and to act with life-affirming agency, is the radical outlaw this nation fears. When he is able to come out of the shadows and subterranean cultures where he already resides and everyone collectively acknowledges his presence, all black males will be able to chart a redemptive sexuality, one that is life-affirming and life-sustaining, a sexuality that no one can give and no one can take away. When he is able to openly choose a healthy sexuality, all black men will claim and celebrate their unalienable rights to know sexual healing, erotic self-expression, and liberated sexual agency.

Chapter 6

from angry boys to angry men

Today many black males in our society embrace the notion that they are victims, that racism, The Man, treacherous black women, bitches of all colors and so forth are all making it hard for them to get ahead. Listening to black male complaints one hears again and again scenarios of disappointment and failure wherein someone else is always to blame. Scapegoating is a diversionary tactic. It allows the scapegoater to avoid the issues they must confront if they are to assume responsibility for their lives. Most black males have consistently received contradictory messages from society about what it means to be responsible. Patriarchal socialization says you are responsible if you get a job, bring your wages home, and provide for your family's material well-being. Yet poverty and a lack of job opportunities have prevented many black males from being responsible in the patriarchal sense of the term. Many black males accept this definition of responsible manhood and spend their lives feeling like a failure, feeling as though their self-esteem is assaulted and assailed on all sides, because they cannot acquire the means to fulfill this role.

Very few black males dare to ask themselves why they do not rebel against the racist, sexist staus quo and invent new ways of thinking about manhood, about what it means to be responsible, about what it means to invent one's life. Often black males are unable to think creatively about their lives because of their uncritical acceptance of narrow life-scripts shaped by patriarchal thinking. Yet individual black men provide models that show it is possible to go against the grain, to change the conventional script. The failure of black males to look to those black males who have liberated themselves via new life maps is rooted in misguided allegiance to the status quo—an allegiance that is cultivated during childhood.

Most black males are bombarded in early childhood with the message that they are inhabiting an all-powerful universe that not only does not want them to succeed but wants to ensure their demise. These messages come to black males via mass media. But even before mass media get a chokehold on the black male psyche, most black boys are conditioned to be victims by emotional abuse, experienced at home and at school. Oftentimes the patriarchal socialization that insists boys should not express emotions or have emotional caretaking is most viciously and ruthlessly implicated in the early childhood socialization of black boys. The image of emasculated and castrated black males is so embedded in the cultural imagination that many black parents feel it is crucial to train boys to be "tough." Houston A. Baker, Jr., in his autobiographical essay "On the Distinction of 'Jr.,'" describes the psychological terrorism that is involved in socializing black boys to patriarchal thinking:

> I am eleven years old, giddy with the joy of fire and awed by the seeming invulnerability of my father. He is removing dead coals from the glowing bed of the furnace. He is risking the peril of

flames. We are sharing . . . we are together. . . . For some reason I am prompted to move with the pure spirit of being. I begin dancing around the furnace with light abandon. My voice slides up the scale to a high falsetto. I am possessed by some primitive god of fire; I feel joyful and secure. I am supremely happy, high-voiced, fluid. Then I am suddenly flattened against a limestone wall, bolts of lightening and bright stars flashing in my head. I have been hard and viciously slapped in the mouth as a thunder-ous voice shouts . . . "Stop acting like a sissy."

Baker calls this violent response from his dad "moods of man-hood." In actuality the young boy is the celebrant expressing love of maleness. It is the adult black male who decides this must be squashed in the name of patriarchal manhood.

This initiating trauma happens to many black boys. Often the abuser is a mother who fears that her son will be "too soft" if he is allowed to be in touch with his feelings. *Soul murder* is the psychological term that best describes this crushing of the male spirit in boyhood. Enlightened therapist Terrence Real, in his book *How Can I Get Through to You?*, shares that the way boys are socialized is fundamentally damaging. In his work-shops all around the country he hears "a hunger for the way out of the dilemma" of patriarchal masculinity. He writes that little has changed in terms of what is expected of boys: "The latest research on boys and their development tells us that, despite our raised consciousness and good intentions, boys today, no less than ever before, are permeated with an inescapable set of highly constricting rules. Those boys who dare to 'step out of the box' place themselves in harm's way since, even today, our cultural tolerance for young men who deviate from what we deem masculine is limited, and our intolerance expressed in singularly ugly ways. . . . The consequence of opposition is psy-chological and often physical brutality." In recent years a num-ber of books have been published which talk about the neces-sity of "protecting the emotional life of boys." When the book jackets have an image, it is usually of a white boy, gazing out at the world with tender wide-open eyes. Any mention in these books of the circumstances surrounding black boys and the processes by which they are socialized is rare.

Undoubtedly white boys, across all classes, are damaged by patriarchal socialization, yet that damage is intensified in the experience of black boys precisely because these boys face a situation of double jeopardy. It is not just society's investment in patriarchal masculinity that demands that black boys be socialized away from feeling and action; they must also bear the weight of a psychohistory that represents black males as castrated, ineffectual, irresponsible, and not real men. It is as if black parents, cross-class, believe they can write the wrongs of history by imposing onto black boys a more brutal indoctrination into patriarchal thinking.

Young black males, like all boys in patriarchal culture, learn early that manhood is synonymous with the domination and control over others, that simply by being male they are in a position of authority that gives them the right to assert their will over others, to use coercion and/or violence to gain and maintain power. Black boys who do not want to be dominant are subjected to forms of psychological terrorism as a means of forcing them to embody patriarchal thinking. Shaming and rituals of disregard, of constant humiliation, are the tactics deployed to break the boy's spirit. Describing how this process works, therapist John Bradshaw writes: "This poisonous pedagogy justifies highly abusive methods for suppressing children's vital spontaneity: physical beatings, lying, duplicity, manipulation, scare tactics, withdrawal of love, isolation and coercion to the point of torture. All of these methods are toxically shaming." Black boys are daily victimized by toxic shaming. In our culture there is very little concern about the emotional lives of black boys.

Even though the welfare of boys began to to receive more attention in this nation as boys committed more violent social acts, particularly murder, the violent acting out of white boys tends to be viewed as a psychological disorder that can be corrected, while black boys who act out tend to be viewed as criminals and punished accordingly. Conservative responses from diverse black communities began to talk about black males as an endangered species. By choosing an animal analogy they embraced racist/sexist iconography that had historically depicted the black male as a beast. Then they focused attention on the need to "civilize" unruly black boys through strict discipline at home and in schools, thus revealing the extent to which they internalized racist/sexist thinking about black masculinity, and paid no meaningful attention to the psychological well-being of black boys. If a black boy obeys authority, is quiet, and does his homework, he tends to be viewed as psychologically whole simply because he is not a problem. Repressed emotions in black boys tend to be viewed not as a problem but as a boon to society since the quiet obedient black boy will know his place and stay in it.

Soul-murdering attacks on the self-esteem of black boys leads many gifted black male children to develop deep-seated chronic depression, resulting from what Bradshaw diagnoses as a consequence of their "true and authentic selves being shamed through abandonment in childhood." In our household growing up, my brother, the one boy in a household with six sisters, was constantly shamed and humiliated by our father for not measuring up to the standards of patriarchal maleness. When he was hurt our brother wanted to cry but the standards of real manliness as our dad envisioned it required that he deny his feelings. Whenever our brother did not conform to patriarchal expectations he was subjected to verbally abusive shaming or violent beatings by our patriarchal father. Like many black boys he received mixed messages about manhood. On one hand he was valued and indulged because he was the boy, and on the other hand he was shamed for not measuring up to some rigid notion of acceptable patriarchal boyhood. He was adored, yet found wanting, and his self-esteem was never allowed to flourish. Like most boys he was rewarded only when he conformed to the patriarchal norm. He could not receive affirmation for simply being.

He was supposed to be obedient and quiet, yet at the same time assertive, aggressive, and able to take control on demand. He was supposed to show affection when adults demanded it and yet not show feelings. These contradictory demands are part and parcel of the complex expectations placed on black boys to show they are not "sissies" but real men in the process of becoming. Their bewilderment at the inconsistency of these demands leads to overwhelming feelings of powerlessness. They feel psychically impotent because they cannot satisfy the demand to "be a man" that adults are placing on them.

Black boys, more than other group of male children in this society, are asked to surrender their childhoods in order to pursue an elusive patriarchial masculinity. Often this demand is made by a dysfunctional single female parent who has had all her expectations of being cared for and protected by a patriarchal male dashed; a disappointing father, a betraying love, both are part of her abandonment issues. She then projects them onto the son who she hopes will fulfill all her desires. These unrealistic emotional expectations result in "emotional sexual abuse"—the conflation that occurs when a child is forced to meet the covert needs of the family system. The general perception that adult black males, particularly those outside the privileged class, are no good dogs who abandon their families is so commonplace that it is acceptable for adult black women to expect boy children to be "mama's little man." Bradshaw clearly states in *Healing the Shame That Binds You* that when this happens "parents are getting their needs met at the expense of the child's needs." When the child's needs are not being met he receives the message that his needs are not important, that he is not valued or worthy. Bradshaw contends that the child then "loses a sense of [his] own personal value."

Among black male children, those who learn in early childhood, long before confronting a hostile white world, that they are not worthy will then encounter that same message when they go out into the public world. Thus they are trapped. They are not valued in family life and they are not valued in the world beyond. Often black male children hear adult women repeatedly maligning adult black males, saying things like "he's no good," "he ain't shit," or "there's not a black man on this earth you can count on." All these messages reinforce the notion that he is flawed, that nothing he can do will make him be whole. All he is offered is a life of compensation, where he must work hard to make up for the "lack" others see in him and for his own sense of inner emptiness.

This core of shame—the shaky foundation on which many black boys must try to construct a self—always collapses. Yet most black males cannot confront the collapse so they focus on performing, on doing rather than being, hiding their deep-seated feelings of hopelessness. Rigid sex roles have provided the backdrop for much of the childhood shaming that wounded black male children are forced to endure. They are the targets of adults who direct their anger and their sense of hopelessness at them. Traumatic emotional abuse happens to black boys of all classes. It may occur repeatedly or it may hit the mark in one soul-destroying act of violation. In Houston Baker's case, though wounded by his father's violent insistence that he not be a sissy, he still feels close to his dad and became an over-achiever, working overtime to show that he is worthy. Baker writes that the admonition to "be a man" was his father's way to communicate that "manhood was a fearless, controlled, purposeful, responsible achievement." Baker was able to actualize his father's vision. His childhood counterpart from an under-class or poor family usually responds to the trauma of being physically abused by emotionally shutting down, by refusing to make any effort to succeed in life. Or if he succeeds he acts out later in life in ways that undermine his success.

Examples abound of professional black men who sabotage their lives for reasons that are not overt. When mass media pay attention to this sabotage there is no discussion of psychological wounding. In recent years when young white males, especially those who have class privilege, violently act out, even killing, psychological issues are explored as possible explanations. Yet when black males act out the message mass media send is that they are "inherently" evil, flawed beyond repair. In even the worst cases, where white males are perceived as committing evil acts (i.e., Jeffrey Dahmer, serial rapists, and killers), immense effort is made to understand their psychological condition, to represent them not as inherently evil but as disturbed. Black male violence is rarely contextualized in this way. During the trial of O.J. Simpson mass-media focus on his childhood was not aimed at providing a sympathetic psychological profile. It was used instead to demonstrate that he was always defective, always a killer in the making, thus reinforcing the racist sexist assumption that all black males are inherently demonic.

That same logic overdetermines racist sexist mass-media reports of black male wrongdoing. Often a symbolic lynching occurs in the press. This was certainly the pattern when Patrick Chavis was murdered. At the age of fifty he was killed in his neighborhood by men seeking to hijack his car. Patrick Chavis was a black student with a grade point average lower than that of many white applicants who were accepted into a California medical school in the early seventies. Chavis's admission became the basis for a lawsuit known as the Bakke case, which was the first major challenge to affirmative action measures that redressed the past and made it possible for underprivileged black students to enter colleges. Raised by a poor single mother of four, Chavis finished medical school and was a successful doctor, yet he continually acted out in ways that undermined his achievements. The heading of the *New York Times* obituary described him as an "affirmative action figure" then offered a detailed account of his "failings": his divorces, his failure to pay child support, the revoking of his medical license. Since he had once been used by Senator Edward Kennedy as a "perfect example" of how affirmative action works, the *Times* used his death to let the world know how wrong Kennedy was. There is no sympathy for Chavis in the long obituary, no attempt to contextualize his story, no sympathetic psychological profile.

Had there been a psychological profile it would have started with the impact of receiving national attention for not being worthy. It would have made mention of the burdens he faced as a black male from an underprivileged dysfunctional family setting striving to achieve. As is often the case in racially biased media, the failing of an individual black male is not contextualized. Chavis is not accorded any respect by Douglas Martin, his obituary writer. He is simply dehumanized, made to stand as yet another example of how black males fail, even when they are given preferential treatment. There is not the slightest suggestion that the public humiliation Chavis faced early in life played a role in undermining his self-esteem, even though he finished medical school and set up a practice. The conservative media's cannibalization of his dead body, using it solely as a means to swipe at affirmative action, is as tragic an assault as the shots that murdered him. Undoubtedly, Chavis was psychologically wounded. Yet like many black males in America he ran from the pain, choking it down, denying and repressing the problem.

Repression is one of the ways to cope with the pain of abandonment. If black boys and black men do not allow themselves to feel, then they are not able to take responsibility for nurturing their emotional growth; they cannot access the healthy parts of themselves that could empower them to resist. Children can resist the impact of shaming by creating alternative worldviews shaped by imagination or by fixating on role models different from their source relationships. But this can only happen if a child's imagination and creativity are not destroyed. Since cre-

ativity in male children is often viewed as suspect from a patriarchal perspective, those aspects of a black male child's identity
may be shut down for fear they will lead him to be punished.
Observing diverse black family dynamics, I notice that creativity in black male children can be expressed before the age of
five but is viewed as a threat to the assumption of a patriarchal
masculine identity if a boy is emotionally expressive and creative beyond these years.

When small, black boys are often overly indulged, made to
feel both special and entitled, they may not learn any boundaries. Everything they do may be praised. This overindulgence
is often perceived as love or positive caretaking when it is actuality an assault on a child's self-worth, for it teaches the child
grandiosity rather than self-acceptance. Harsh punishment is
often the way dysfunctional parents seek to alter the behavior
of the grandiose child. When the overindulgence ends and the
shaming begins, the child can garner attention only for negative
behaviors. He cannot stop acting out because aggression is the
way he gets noticed. Craving attention and only getting it when
he is "bad," he sees no way to gain enough affirmation to feel
good about himself. Concurrently, he may learn that if he
represses aggression and any other emotional feelings that
make adults uncomfortable, he will be treated better. What little affirmation and attention he receives will come only if he is
seen as performing well in the eyes of adults.

This need to prove their value through performance is one
of the reasons so many black boys look to sports as a site of
redemption and affirmation. Given the history of black male
success in the arena of sports, an arena deemed "manly" by
patriarchal standards, black boys learn early on in their lives
that by excelling in sports they can gain both visibility and a
measure of respect. Acting out the patriarchal paradigm as
competitive performers, black boys who excel at sports are able
to shield themselves from the shaming and scorn directed at
the boy who expresses his creativity in academic or artistic pur-

suits. However, black boys who do not find their way to sports or are unable to succeed playing sports have little or no opportunity to regain lost self-respect. Black boys who are repeatedly subjected to humiliations, shaming, embarrassments, or random punishments by grown ups learn that they can relieve this pain by repression and dissociation. Acting out violently is another way to take control of the pain. In *Lost Boys: Why Our Sons Turn Violent and How We Can Save Them*, therapist James Garbarino explores the link between the harsh repression of boys during the ages when they are emotionally vulnerable and later violent acting out. He found that such boys were often labeled from birth as difficult or as too demanding. Labeled as "terrors" they became just that. He explains: "Without loving guidance, spiritual counsel, and psychological nurturance, children see little alternative to cope as best as they can, and that generally means disassociation—no matter its cost to a child's inner life." In general our society does not care about the inner life of black boys. When the emotional abandonment that is more often than not their lot in life leads to dysfunctional behavior, black boys get noticed but rarely in a manner that positively addresses their issues.

Emotionally abused black boys are filled with rage. Primed to act out they become adults who are rageoholics. There is often so much attention given the concrete material manifestations of the impact of racism and other forms of social oppression on black males that the psychological impact of early childhood abandonment is not highlighted. Yet the powerlessness that many black males feel in childhood continues into adulthood. Gary Zukav and Linda Francis, in *The Heart of the Soul*, identify lack of self-worth as the core cause of anger: "It is the experience of powerlessness. Powerlessness is seeing yourself as valueless, as not being able to imagine that you make a difference to anyone or anything. . . . When you feel worthless, you are terrified by your life, and when you are terrified by your life, you are continually in the pain of trying to shape your life as you think it needs to be. When that pain is acute, you cover it with anger." Many black males in our nation are consumed by rage. Continually angry, they are in continual pain. And this is one of the reasons they look for scapegoats.

Zukav and Francis state: "Anger lashes out at a target. That target is another person, group of people, or the Universe. Anger is righteous and self-important. Anger does not listen to, respect, or care about others. It makes others wrong, to blame, inferior, or inadequate. It cares only about itself. Anger wants what it wants, when it wants it, on the terms that it wants it. It assumes the roles of judge, jury, and executioner. There is no appeal." The chronically angry black male is living in an emotional prison. Fear-based, he is isolated and terrified. In patriarchal culture his anger may be seen as "manly," so it becomes the perfect cover-up so that no one, not even himself, can know the extent of the pain he feels. John Bradshaw sheds light on the way rage often makes the wounded self feel better: "When we are raging, we feel unified within—no longer split. We feel powerful. Everyone cowers in our presence. We no longer feel inadequate and defective. As long as we can get away with it, our rage becomes our mood altered of choice. We become rage addicts." Black male rage is often interpreted as a positive response to injustice and as a consequence it is encouraged. In actuality black male rage is usually a sign of reactive powerlessness. It rarely leads to constructive intervention. Raging further shames and isolates black men. Addiction is often seen as a way to find sanctuary, a way out of the feelings of powerlessness. Richard Pryor chronicles this in an insightful manner in the autobiographically based film *Jo Jo Dancer, Your Life Is Calling*. His character splits into two parts: one that speaks the powerlessness, and one the drug-addicted user who speaks back with a false sense of power. Pryor powerfully portrays the dissociative states black males often inhabit.

Substance abuse is a way black men attempt to contain and control their rage. It keeps the pain at bay, it seems to temper the rage. In *Brothers on the Mend* Ernest Johnson writes: "Many black men prefer to suppress their anger and rage suffering the consequences, rather than open up and talk about their feelings. These 'cool brothers' express their angry feelings in a number of nonproductive ways—overuse of tobacco, drowning the bile through drinking, or releasing the welled-up feelings in a burst of violence—often against loved ones. Talking through the feelings is not seen as an option because they want to appear strong and 'manly.' But understanding the forces that cause sudden, even murderous rage—and more important, learning how to manage and control the impulse, may be the most important factors in the survival of African-American men." Chronic anger needs to be eliminated, not managed. Many black females learn to cope in a society that denies us full access to forms of power without acting out murderous rage, and black males can learn the same survival kills. Rageoholism in black males cannot be addressed if black males are unable to express their pain due to patriarchal repression. The pain underlying the anger causes the feelings of powerlessness, of sadness.

Rage is the perfect cover-up for depression. Black males who feel powerless, who feel as though they are not able to bring any level of meaningful purpose to their lives, are often depressed. That depression may be the outcome of unreconciled grief. In mourning for the self that has not come into being, sad about repeated failure and ongoing loss, depressed black men fade into the background in our society. Their problems go unnoticed. There are few avenues for healing that are open to them.

Ultimately in imperialist white-supremacist capitalist patriarchy black male rage is acceptable, expected even. No one really wants to hear black men speak their pain or offer them avenues of healing. Even though Ellis Cose reveals tremendous compassion for himself and other black men in *The Envy of the World*, he does not make the connection between low self-worth and self-sabotage. Instead he writes: "It would, of course, be simplistic—and wrong—to try to reduce all our problems . . . to issues of self-esteem or self-worth. There are other huge problems, and perhaps none is larger than those that revolve around abandonment." Cose fails to see the link between abandonment in childhood and lifelong debilitating low self-esteem. Yet this is the core issue for black males. In actuality, a great many of the problems black males face are a consequence of feeling that they have no value.

Lack of self-esteem—the consequence of psychological wounding in early childhood—is the heart of the matter. And when those wounds are not healed they invariably lead to self-sabotage. Often in our nation folks ponder why professional educated black males who are "successful" act out in the same self-sabotaging ways as their less-educated economically disenfranchised counterparts. Like Cose, they seem not to recognize that the core lack of self-worth is the same for overachievers and underachievers. Male success in patriarchal society tends to be measured by material standards (how much money a man makes, what kind of car he drives, or even the looks of the babe on his arm). This leads folks to forget that one can have the outer trappings of material success, even wealth and fame, and still feel an inner emptiness, an ongoing feeling of loss. Until wounded black males are able to confront the emotional abuse in their childhood (abuse is always about abandonment) they will not know emotional well-being.

Working on the issue of male violence, Donald Dutton acknowledges that the "way out of this miasma of unrealistic expectation and cyclical disappointment," the trapped feelings of powerless which engender rage, begins with acknowledging and feeling the pain. After breaking through the wall of denial black males who seek healing must do the work of grieving. They must, like all wounded males, "mourn the loss of what was never attained and attempt to integrate the good and bad aspects of what is still possible," as Dutton suggests. He points out that most men refuse to acknowledge deep childhood losses, and that "male models for grieving are few." In traditional patriarchal black culture, male grieving has no place. The black man who grieves is seen as weak. Oftentimes the only black male we see expressing grief (other than at a funeral) is the drunk whose emotionality is dismissed as caused merely by his addiction and not by pain.

In *The Batterer* Donald Dutton states: "Men in particular seem incapable of grieving and mourning on an individual basis. Perhaps that is why the blues are so popular with men. They serve a socially sanctioned form of expression for this lost and unattainable process." Black men created the blues. articulating in song their pain, their sense of hopelessness, their lamentation. For those individual creators the blues was a way out of the pain. It let them express their sorrow without shame. For men who listen while denying their own anguish, the sense of hopelessness remains. Young black males tend not to want to hear the blues. They do not want to hear an honest emotional expression of black male vulnerability. They would rather hear rap music with its aggressive presentation of invulnerability. If the choice is between exposing the true authentic self and clinging to the false self, most males maintain their fantasy bonding rather than seek the real. Although they like to use the phrase "keeping it real" most black males are too caught up in false selves, too busy dissimulating (taking on any appearance to manipulate) to recognize the "real."

Resisting the patriarchal masculinity that preconditions men to be mentally imbalanced, that serves as a breeding ground for pathology, is one path to wellness any black male can take. Too often black males confuse whining, complaining, and raging with resistance. Constructive resistance names the problems, affirms the ways folks are victimized and hurt, while also mapping strategies for healing. Imperialist white-supremacist capitalist patriarchy reinforces the pathological narcissism that keeps many black men trapped by their identification with being a victim. Excessive focus on the ways racism wounds black male spirits is often evoked to deflect attention away from all other sources of emotional pain. That deflection is disempowering because it sends the message that there is nothing black males can do to create positive change since they are "powerless" to end white supremacy. Racism does damage black males, but so does sexism, so does class elitism with its hedonistic materialism, and so does abandonment and abuse in family relationships. All the sources of black male pain and powerlessness must be named if healing is to take place, if black males are to reclaim their agency.

Wounded black men can heal. The healing process requires that they break through denial, feel what they feel, and tell the truth. In recovery work the often-evoked phrase "you are only as sick as your secrets" is insightful. A culture of domination is always one that prefers lies over truth. Black males who lie—to themselves, to everyone in their lives—are unable to experience the integrity that is essential to emotional well-being, that is the core of healthy self-esteem. Lies do not work. Telling the truth is the way to heal. Nothing stands in the way of any black male taking this step in the direction of well-being. He simply needs to seek salvation. The root meaning of *salvation* is "wholeness." As black males courageously confront the pain in their lives, facing reality, they can take the broken bits and pieces and make themselves whole again.

Chapter 7

waiting for daddy to come home

---

black male parenting

Males in our nation do very little parenting. Yet we hear so much about the importance of having a man in the house. The absent man, the absent father, has been the constant sign folks point to when they want to critique black families. This is especially the case when those critiques are coming from unenlightened white folks. No matter the presence of overwhelming research and data about the patriarchal white nuclear family, which documents that it has never been a safe place for women or children, unenlightened white folks still represent this configuration as the only truly healthy family system. In our segregated black world, as children we learned about white families from television. The white fathers we saw on shows like *Leave It to Beaver*, *Father Knows Best*, and *The Courtship of Eddie's Father* were kind protectors and providers who gave their children unconditional love. They did not yell, beat, shame, ignore, or wound their children. They were the fantasy white family. The real white family, the ones where fathers were controlling, abusive, incestuous, violent, alcoholics, workaholics, or rage-oholics, did not appear on our television screens.

These were the family images of fathers in the fifties and sixties. None of the white fathers who entertained us on our television screens were patriarchal male dominators. They were patriarchal (in that they conformed to sexist defined roles) but they were benevolent. Finally in the eighties we got our own African-American version of the fantasy dapper dad on *The Cosby Show*. Lovable, kind, a protector, and a provider, our fantasy black dad was funny; he had the ability to eliminate pain by making us laugh. There was never any rage or abuse or emotional neglect of any kind on *The Cosby Show*. No wonder, then, so many black children fell in love with the fantasy father and longed for him to come and take us away from our real fathers who seemed not to know how a father should act—what he should feel, be, and do. That longing for the fantasy father was even more intense in single-parent female-headed households. With no real father to disturb the idealized fantasy, fatherless sons and daughters could and do pretend that if only there was a man in the house, a father, everything would be perfect; they would be happy.

When black pundits, whether political figures or intellectuals, talk about the black family, they too seem to buy into the romantic myth that if only there was a black man in the house life would be perfect. Like children, who know no better, they refuse to accept the evidence that there are plenty of homes where fathers are present, fathers who are so busy acting out, being controlling, being abusive, that home is hell, and children in those homes spend lots of time wishing the father would go away. The father-hunger these children feel is as intense as the father-hunger children in fatherless homes feel. Patriarchal fathers are not the answer to healing the wounds in black family life. Ultimately it is more important that black children have loving homes than homes where men are present. Psychologically healthy, loving single mothers and fathers raise healthy children. Dysfunctional homes where there is no love, where mother and father are present but abusive are just as damaging as dysfunctional single-parent homes.

Children need loving fathers and/or loving male parental caregivers. Fathers who are not present all the time can still be a loving presence. Concurrently the presence of biological fathers matters less than the presence of loving black male parental caregivers. These father figures shape the vision children have of who black men are and can be. Since patriarchal culture overvalues the two-parent family, representing it as the ideal, all children in the nation who are raised in families that do not resemble this ideal have to be taught that their families are not defective. Children in homes where fathers are not present need to be taught that there is no "lack" that renders them flawed. This does not negate the reality that every child needs to experience connection with loving adult women and men, that children (even those created from sperm donations) want to know who their fathers are, and if the father can be known they want to encounter him. This will always be the case as long as the two-parent family is presented to children as the ideal.

Many black children are emotionally neglected and/or abandoned by biological fathers. Identifying the issue of father abandonment as a serious problem in *The Envy of the World* Ellis Cose states: "Today the vast majority of black children don't live with both parents. A few decades ago that was not the case. In 1960, just over two thirds of black children under the age of eighteen lived in a household with two parents. By 1991, the percentage had dropped to just over one third—and has continued going down since. The implications of that are staggering. For what it means, among other things, is that a lot of black children—more than ever—feel that at least one parent, generally the father, has abandoned them." Reading this quote one might assume that if black fathers were in the home they would be doing the work of parenting; this is simply not the case.

Women in our nation continue to do the lion's share of parenting. As a consequence children feel emotional abandonment in both homes where fathers are present and homes where they are absent. Obviously, in a healthy two-parent household fathers do not emotionally neglect children, but most families are dysfunctional. The patriarchal norm, which teaches men that child care and parental caregiving is woman's work, continues to prevail despite feminist research that indicates that children are healthier when emotionally nurtured by both female and male parents. Since so many black males uncritically accept patriarchal thinking, they continue to believe that children do not need a father's care as much as they need mothers. This faulty logic, reinforced by patriarchal norms, persists even though it is more than apparent that children need to be nurtured by fathers, long for father love, and without it suffer. Boys and girls need to be loved by adult men. It is not essential to their well-being that these men be biological fathers, rather that they offer a child the opportunity to be affirmed and loved by an adult male parental caregiver. Boys, especially, need adult men to be role models to teach them how to negotiate the patriarchy in ways that are not soul damaging, to show them how to work around the system, and to create healthy alternative self-concepts.

In the collection *Father Songs: Testimonies by African-American Sons and Daughters* there are few contributors who do not know or have never interacted with their fathers. This fact reminds us that the underlying issue is less the absence of fathers and more the painful lack of emotional engagement by fathers, whether they are continually present or not. No matter the huge amount of evidence documenting the damaging impact of loveless father-child relationships; most black people continue to believe that fathers do not matter as much as mothers. Parenting is a difficult, arduous, time-consuming job that men are not eager to do. In this way black males are no exception. From slavery on many black males have chosen to avoid parenting. They breed children they have no intention of raising. Colluding with black women who have been brainwashed by patriarchal thinking, they believe that father-love is not essential to a child's well being. To address in any meaningful way the issue of emotional neglect of children by black fathers, we must first acknowledge the fact that many black folks believe fathers play no meaningful role in a child's life. Paradoxically, folks continue to hold this belief even in the face of overwhelming evidence to the contrary.

Perhaps the belief that male parenting is not relevant continues to be a norm in black life because it obscures the reality that so many black men are biological fathers who have no desire to parent. Until black people of all classes are able to place value on the active participation of black males in parenting, black boys and young men will continue to believe that their purpose is simply to sire children, that they prove their manhood in a patriarchal sense by making babies, not by taking care of them.

In *Father Songs* grown children of absent fathers testify about the ways they were wounded by the emotional neglect of fathers. Black males talk about punishment and physical abuse at the hands of fathers who betrayed trust. In Scott Minerbrook's essay, "My Father, Myself," he writes of fearing that "I wasn't worthy of my father's love, that I was not valuable to him." He confesses: "Even though I loved him, my love was mixed with fear that any small happiness I might feel could be snatched away if exposed to him. So many years later, I see him as someone much like myself. Someone who grew up, as many of his generation did, unable to show weakness, unable to express his pain except in acts of violence. . . . Unable to acknowledge his own emotions, my father could never allow others to show emotion, and his murderous rage became the mold upon which I shaped my world." Minerbrook's fear is echoed in countless testimonies about the nature of black father-child relationships.

Each one of my siblings feels a love for our dad that continues to be mixed with fear. We were raised to admire our patriarchal dad because he provided for us and protected us (a euphemism for his capacity to be violent). But in becoming this man who inspired fear, he had to remain emotionally distant. In our household of six daughters and one son, our brother was the most deeply affected by our dad's judgment and disapproval of his vulnerable, burgeoning manhood. Boys shamed by fathers struggle to find self-worth. Even though our father was always in the home, and is still there after fifty years of marriage to our mother, for most of that time he was emotionally unavailable. Now in his early eighties our father talks with us, expresses his feelings, and gives care. When he first began to reach out, to make emotional connections, we were reluctant to respond. Like many patriarchal households, ours was one where Dad and Mom were and are often at odds. During our childhoods, our mother's subjugation filled us with rage. And like many children we often felt we had to prove our loyalty to her by distancing ourselves from Dad and from our desire to know and love him. He tried to bridge that distance by being critical of Mom, which just made us all the more disappointed in him.

It took years for me to work on forgiving Dad his emotional neglect and his acts of abuse. When I began to forgive him, I was able to recover joyous memories, to value the positive aspects of his being. Speaking with black folks whose fathers were brutal and/or continually emotionally abusive I find that one part of the process, one way to heal the wounds of separation from fathers, is the conscious re-remembering of what we liked about our fathers. It seems that gender difference makes it easier for black females to approach our fathers and talk about the lack of emotional connection. Since Dad was always harder on our brother, always making him feel worthless, it has been difficult for him to reconcile with Dad. Minerbrook states: "I hunger also for the language of reconciliation, which does not seem to exist between many Black men who are like me and their fathers who are like mine. Our wounds seem to run too deep. . . . This lack of language between African-American men most often seems a cultural flaw. The issue of the wounds African-American fathers unwittingly bring into their relationships with their children influences every aspect of our lives. It influences everything from how we perceive our relationship to authority, to our capacities for harm or for good." Like all men, black men in patriarchal culture have not been raised to be intimate. Therapist Terrence Real suggests that wounded men confronting the prospect of intimacy often become flooded "with pain, mistrust, and fear," all of which are triggered by feelings of shame. Men, says Real, often seek to cover up emotional vulnerability by moving from helplessness to dominance and transmuting pain into rage. Most black folks remember their father's rage and/or contempt and this is the traumatic bond that fuels pain and shame.

I hear many stories of individuals raised in households headed by single females who first learn the identify of their absent fathers by hearing adult female gossip or they are informed of his identity carelessly by a neighbor or stranger. Often when they share with their mothers the desire to establish connection with absent fathers, these adult females respond angrily. Often, grown women who are enraged by male refusal to assume responsibility for parenting resent children for longing to make connections with fathers. This resentment adds to a child's emotional confusion. *Father Songs* opens with a chapter entitled "Are You My Father?" Charmagne Helton writes: "A stocky man walked up to me and kissed me on the cheek and as he held me tight, smiling and looking into my face, I was terrified. I had no idea who he was. . . . There were no introductions. He just kept squeezing. As soon as I could get free from him, I ran down the church steps to my mother." When she asked her mother the identity of the man who frightened her, she was told, "That's your daddy." This moment of fleeting recognition is a story many black folks can tell. And more often than not it was a moment filled with a sense of violation, of unwanted intrusion. One woman remembers riding in a car, seeing a man staring from his car, asking her grandmother "Who is that man?" and being told he was her father. And that was it: no discussion, no processing. Most of the anger at these encounters is directed at the father because children are unable to see the mother's collusion, her tacit acceptance that knowing one's father is unimportant.

In too many cases single black mothers, especially those who are teenagers when they give birth, may not want children to have contact with their fathers. His emotional abandonment of her and his emotional and/or material abandonment of the family may lead her to feel he has no role to play in her child's life. Writing in *Soul Babies* about gendered warfare in the essay "Baby Mama (Drama) and Baby Daddy (Trauma)," Mark Anthony Neal states that black males who rage at the mother of their children often are scapegoating in order to shield themselves from self-critique, from assuming accountability. He writes: "It is my contention that the baby mama has become a singular trope employed to explain the absence of black fathers and the loss of a meaningful patriarchy/masculinity that also condones modes of violence, both physically and rhetorically, against black women for their roles in diminishing these entities within the black community. . . . Ironically many critiques of the baby mama obscure the more powerful role of the state in the removal of black men, laying a good portion of the blame on the baby mama." Most black males who father children are not denied access; they simply do not want to parent. When children seek out these "absent fathers" whom they may have felt were kept away by their mother, they learn the true story. They come face to face with willful father abandonment. The father-hunger they feel rarely connects with a child-hungry father who is eager to know and nourish his children.

Oftentimes absent fathers encountering children for the first time behave as though they are children themselves—like the father who cannot speak to his child, who cannot identify himself, owning his own relationship. One explanation for black male abandonment of children is simply that failure to heal the wounded child within usually means that when the adult who has never recovered from loss and abandonment in his own childhood, who has buried the pain, has a child, the presence of the child acts as a trigger for the pain. Getting away from the child, he escapes the remembered pain. In "An Open Letter to My Dad" Charlie Braxton tells the story of his father babysitting him and his baby brother yet spending the time packing up every item in the house. He simply leaves the children alone. Braxton recalls: "When I asked you what you were doing with all of our stuff, you told me that we were moving to a brand new home and that you would be right back to get us after you had put everything up. . . . It was three years before I saw you again. I was still waiting for you to come and take us all to our new home. It never happened." Now, this adult black male may have been absolutely focused on hurting his wife, but the children were the casualties in this war; they were the ones traumatically wounded. Braxton shares that he grew up thinking he was the reason his father left. That internalized blame caused him to suffer. Yet when he has children Braxton recognizes that he needs to heal these old wounds with his dad in order to fully grow up, and he is not ashamed to say to his dad, "I need you now, more than I ever did when I was growing up."

John Bradshaw points out that "all parents who have not worked through their own childhood trauma will reenact it on their own children." Many adult black males were victimized in childhood by paternal and maternal sadism. Then, when they become parents and see themselves enacting the same rituals of disregard and disrespect that traumatically wounded them, they feel overwhelmed by shame. Some of these men feel that exiting from their child's life is the best thing they can do.

I hear black folks whose fathers have failed to give adequate recognition proudly testify that they refuse to forgive those fathers later on when they come seeking to make amends. Often, absent fathers will reappear late in life when they are sick or dying. Yet their longing for reconciliation still matters and should be seriously considered. It is clear that we hunger for moments of reconciliation and reunion because forgiveness, reestablishing connections, or forging bonds that were never present helps us all heal. When I wrote a letter to my dad openly expressing my feelings about him, my childhood longing for the affirmation from him that never came, he was open and receptive. My mother was the person who responded with hostility, whose faulty Christian-based notions of forgiveness, precluded direct confrontation and demanded that the one who hurt us make amends. Although she attempted to shame me for wanting to speak with Dad about our relationship, he did not. He never really talked with me about the content of the letter, but he read it and our communication improved. In the letter I let him know that I loved him. Because of their own childhood experiences many black males who never knew a father's care cannot imagine how much their care matters to children. (My Dad's mom was emotionally unavailable even though she doted on him, and the only parental relationship he developed was with his biological father who was married to someone else as an adult.)

Therapist Terrence Real suggests that there are five self-skills that constitute adult maturity, and if these "healthy capacities were not present in our early relationships, they will be missing in our personalities." They are self-esteem (holding the self in warm regard), self-awareness (knowing one's own experience and sharing it), boundaries (self-protecting yet able to connect with others), interdependence (identifying needs and wants, caring for self yet able to receive care from others), and moderation (experiencing and expressing oneself moderately). Most black males have not been taught these skills. Because they form the psychological foundation needed for healthy parenting it is important for black males to acquire these skills. Yet they are skills that are at odds with the patriarchal requirements for manhood. To acquire them, then, a man must let go patriarchy's hold on his consciousness. He must be and do things differently. For black males this means daring to create new life scripts. It requires daring to cultivate the courage to heal. Thaddeus Goodavage reveals in his essay "Are You My Father?" that he has the courage when he openly declares that "the need and potential in my soul to father and be fathered, had to be nurtured and made real" because "I was so paralyzed with feelings of such a deep loneliness and worthlessness that I was unable to understand why I was a valuable person and why I should try to remain alive."

Trapped by dehumanizing toxic shame, wounded black males must do the work of reclaiming their past in order to live fully in the present. To heal themselves they must come out of hiding and take the risk of forging emotional connections that are not shaming. Goodavage came to the realization that "I needed help." From there he began the process of self-discovery, "asking myself about my family life, asking myself about how I was fathered, forcing myself to remember my pain is about my beginning to heal." Confronting their childhoods and early relationships, looking at what they were taught and how the lessons learned affected their sense of themselves and others, wounded black males can begin to heal the hurt, to come out of isolation and let themselves live again.

Imagine if, instead of a public spectacle of black men gathering in a "day of atonement" like the Million Man March, black males had been asked to have a week of healing where they establish connection, make amends, and do the work of forgiveness with the folks in their lives they have wounded. Imagine a four-day program that begins with black males making peace with their source figures, then with their loved ones, then with friends they have wounded, and finally reaffirming bonds with themselves. Again and again patriarchal thinking tells men that what they do outside the home is more important than what they do inside the home. This is one of the reasons most black males cannot take being a parent seriously. Far too many black males and females think that all a father needs to do is give money. While material support is one way to demonstrate care, it can never take the place of emotional bonding, of caring and loving interaction.

In the anti-patriarchal practice of parenting what is deemed most important for any child is that they be given love. Fathers can love their children whether they are present on a full-time basis are not. Unlike patriarchal thinking, which insists that the presence of a father is needed in family life because men are superior protectors and providers, healthy parenting is rooted in the assumption that because we live in a world where there are two genders, children need to be able to make emotional connections with both the male and the female. Those connections can rightly begin at birth or in early childhood. If fathers are present and loving, then they are a wonderful source of this positive connection, and if they are not present, children benefit greatly from having loving adult male parental caregivers. In female-headed households that are healthy, where loving mothers are wise, mothers know they need to provide models of healthy adult maleness for their children. Providing this is the way they create a functional loving home. Acknowledging the value of a loving adult male presence in a child's life should not negate the reality that healthy children, male and female, are and can be raised in homes where there is not a male present all the time.

A healthy loving father or adult male parental caregiver who assumes a fathering role demonstrates his care in the same manner as mothers do. When men share equally in parenting or do single parenting, fatherhood is recognized as having that same meaning and significance. More than enough evidence exists (particularly in the data on child abuse) to demonstrate that the biological experience of pregnancy and childbirth does not make women's parenting superior to men's. The testimony of men who are parenting alone reveals that they nurture in ways that are akin to that of female parents. In the essay on "Revolutionary Parenting" in *Feminist Theory: From Margin to Center*, I emphasize the need to place the same value on fatherhood that we do on motherhood: "Dictionary definitions of the word 'father' relate its meaning to accepting responsibility, with no mention of words like 'tenderness' and 'affection' yet these words are used to define what the word 'mother' means. By placing sole responsibility for nurturing—that is to say for satisfying the emotional and material needs of children onto women—society reinforces the notion that to mother is more important than to father. . . . Women and men must define the work of fathering and mothering in the same way if males and females are to accept equal responsibility in parenting. . . . There should be a concept of effective parenting that makes no distinction between maternal and paternal care." The model of effective parenting that includes a vision of attentive love is essential practice for male and female parents.

Often fathers do not learn how to parent because they are still assuming that a father's role is merely to exercise authority and provide for material needs. In patriarchal culture fathers are taught that this role is secondary to the mothering role. When males parent, using the same effective model taught to women, they create healthy homes and healthy children. While the number of black males who abandon children, who turn away from parenting, is increasing daily, it is equally true that among men who parent effectively black males are well represented. Studies of parenting show that poor and working-class men who may hold the sexist belief that parenting is female work often do more parenting. This has been the case for black males.

In the elder phase of his life my Dad has become an important loving parental caregiver for his grandchildren and great grandchildren. He provides the emotional care that he did not give his own children when we were young. As he has aged he has become more aware of the importance of emotional bonding. Seeing this emotional development in a black male patriarch restores my hope. It lets me concretely see that it is never too late for black fathers to do the work of loving parenting. Dad has been changed by doing this work. He has opened the heart that patriarchal manhood told him should stay closed forever. He is the living embodiment of the feminist message that when males do the work of parenting they do the work of becoming whole, bringing together the parts of themselves that patriarchy demanded they sever. They learn to laugh, play, and express emotions. They learn the language of forgiveness and tenderness. They speak sweet words. They become more like those fantasy fathers we admired on our television screens. They become men who can give unconditional love.

Our fathers are important to us. We value them as much as we value our mothers. Rejecting the patriarchal notion that we should value them more because they are male, we value them simply because we love them. We need them because we love them. And it is never too late to speak that love, to invite our fathers to do the work of self-recovery so that they may dance with us in the circle of love. Lurma Backley's autobiographical essay, "My 'Real' Daddy's Girl," reminds readers that, through the practice of loving, a father who is not a biological dad is as "real" a dad as one can be. Sharing the way his respect and love for her and her sister laid the foundation for them to have a healthy vision of black male parenting, Backley writes: "Sometimes people who knew us before Mama and Daddy married would ask us if we ever heard from our 'real' daddy. I thought they were crazy. This was my real daddy. No other man could have, or did, love me more; no other man could have, or did, teach me better lessons, or show me a better model for a man-woman relationship." Real dads have done the work of growing up, of emotional maturation. Real dads give love, that combination of care, commitment, knowledge, responsibility, respect, and trust. They are both born and made.

When all black males learn that fatherhood is less about bio-logical creation than about the capacity to nurture the spiritual and emotional growth of a child's life, then they will teach that lesson to the males who come after them. They will no longer need to run away from home and family to find themselves. They will do the work of self-discovery and self-recovery right where they are, beginning in that place where we all hunger for a fathering presence.

Chapter 8

doing the work of love

Whenever I lecture on love and speak about black male and female relationships audiences always assume that I am talking about romantic bonds. I have to remind them that romantic relationships are just one of the bonds black males and females share, that I am including the relationships between parent and child, brother and sister, and so on. These source relationships—that is, the intimate bonds we make in our family origin—tend to shape the attitudes, habits of being and modes of interacting that we bring to romantic partnerships. Everything we commonly hear about romantic partnerships between black women and men is negative. We hear that black men are dogs and black women bitches and ho's. We hear that the divorce rates are so much higher than those of other groups. We hear about the lying and the cheating and the lowdown violence. We hear about the mistrust and the hatred. We hear that black women are getting more of society's good than black men are, that they are moving ahead and leaving black men behind.

We get the bad news. And it is repeated again and again. It's the stuff movies are based on. It's the stuff of novels and poetry. In popular culture there are a bevy of loudmouths who let us know what goes wrong when black men and women get together. We get books with titles posing the question "Do Black Women Hate Black Men?" or announcing that the "war between the genders" continues.

We do not commonly hear about the black males and females who love each other. We do not hear how they manage to find their way to love when the odds are so stacked against them. We do not hear the ways they establish functional caring black families. The collective silence in our culture about healthy black male and female relationships damages us. It keeps our minds and hearts fixed on all that is not working. It keeps from us the knowledge of what we must do to make relationships work. It keeps many of us looking for the confirmation bias, i.e., we start out with the assumption that no love exists between black women and men, and that is what we find.

Black male and female relationships have had the same difficulties that appear in all relationships in a culture of domination where patriarchal thinking prevails. Yet the way we respond to these difficulties reveals major differences. Unlike mainstream culture, black folks come to one another with the expectation that we will find love but we often bring the added expectation that the relationships we form will undo the damage done by racism. Moreover most black folks have been so concerned with charting the impact of racism in their lives that they fail to examine all the other painful formative traumas that may have little or nothing to do with racism.

Honestly, as black males and females, we are often unable to tell the truth that the vast majority of us are coming out of dysfunctional families and that these early intimate bonds make it difficult for us to achieve emotional maturity and well-being.

The most damaging lie that continues to be told about the black family is that it is dysfunctional because so many of our homes are headed by females. African-American two parent households are as likely to be as dysfunctional as their single parent counterparts. Almost all families of any race are dysfunctional in our society. Because of the added impact of racism, the dysfunctions in African-American life are often more extreme. The core reasons for dysfunction in black families is blind allegiance to patriarchal thinking about sex roles and the coupling of that thinking with rigid fundamentalist religious beliefs. Dominator culture creates family dysfunction.

Again it must be stated that when racism is added to the mix dysfunctions are intensified. Yet racism is not the core issue. We know this because some of us have come through the experiences of dysfunction to healthy wholeness, and the system of racism has remained intact. Concurrently, it has been easier to challenge and change racism in the society than it has been to alter the rigid patriarchal thinking about gender that abounds in black life and is often reinforced by religion. Most black people are anti-racist (even those who have internalized racial self-hatred) and will not argue that whites are better, superior, and should rule over us. Yet most black people are not anti-sexist (even those whose life circumstance may make it impossible for them to rigidly conform to sexist roles) and will argue the natural superiority of men, supporting their right to dominance in the family and in the world outside the home. We learned sex roles and acceptable ways to relate to one another within the family.

That is why no meaningful discussion of black male and female relationships can happen if it does not begin with a discussion of childhood, of what we learned then about appropriate social interaction between black males and females. Therapist John Bradshaw contends: "Our families are the places where we have our source relationships. Families are where we first learn about ourselves in the mirroring eyes of our parents, where we see ourselves for the first time. In families we learn about emotional intimacy. We learn what feelings are and how to express them. Our parents model what feelings are acceptable and family authorized and what feelings are prohibited." In the bosom of the patriarchal two-parent and single-female-headed family many of us learned that men and women were different and that these differences often led to conflict, that men had the right to rule over women and children, that punishment was good, that patriarchal authority was always right and that children really held the same status as slaves whose primary task was to obey. When psychoanalyst Alice Miller wrote about dysfunctional families in *For Your Own Good* she called these unhealthy parenting rules "poisonous pedagogy": "Adults are the masters of the dependent child and determine in a godlike fashion what is right and wrong. The child is held responsible for the anger of adults and parents must always be shielded from facing reality. The child's life-affirming feelings pose a threat to the autocratic parent and therefore the child's will must be broken as soon as possible, preferably at a very early age so that the child is not aware of what happens and will not be able to expose the adults." Whenever these rules are in place violation and abuse will occur. A large majority of black folks have been raised by these poisonous parenting rules and will in adulthood defend them. Because this is so widespread, there is a tacit agreement in many black families that "abuse" is good for the child; it just isn't called abuse. It is called punishment. And the assumption underlying it is that black children are bad and must be disciplined before they get completely out of control. Mostly these rules are enacted without much discussion. In dysfunctional two-parent families women and men do not talk together about the best way to raise children.

Over a period of several years I taught African-American literature in classes with a large number of black students. They were often disturbed by the representations of romantic relationships between black males and females in fiction. When I asked them to describe the communications they had witnessed in their homes between adult black males and females most everyone agreed that they had not really witnessed much conversation between the two groups. I shared with my students that my parents could be in the same room with one another and one would say "tell your mother . . ." or "tell your dad. . . ." Mostly, students described monologues where the person of the opposite sex listened but rarely responded—but no dialogue.

Growing up I learned from my dad's very vocal sexism that men preferred women who did not talk, who listened and obeyed. In those days our mother was not much of a talker, at least when Dad was around. Their sexist thinking about the appropriate roles for women and men were always substantiated by Old Testament teachings, which advanced the notion that women, like children, should be seen and not heard. Gender roles in many two-parent black families continue to be influenced by sexism. Although critics of black male-and-female relationships like to talk about the continued existence of a gender war in black life, as though conflict between the two groups is fueled by feminist revolution, in actuality the cause of most battles is failure to conform adequately to the sexist norms. Most black females are not feminist. Despite the fact that we hear so much about how there are more jobs available for females or that females often make more money than their male counterparts, the reality remains that the desire to have a man who assumes a conventional patriarchal role of manly protector and provider is still the norm. Even though black women work, they fantasize about not working. Or they dream of being able to stop working for a time if there is a man to watch their back. And they want him to be the knight in shining armor ready to defend their honor. No matter that this is the stuff of romantic fantasy, the stuff that gender equality was supposed to do away with. This is the basic longing of many women, including black women: to have a man who will assume the conventional sexist masculine roles.

Concurrently, most black males are not looking for a woman who is a peer; they want a woman who is traditionally feminine as defined by sexist thinking, who subordinates her will to his, who lives to please him. They may support her working as long as she either makes less or turns over her income for him to be the keeper of the family finances. One of the biggest myths about black male-and-female relationships that abounds in this nation is that black women are powerful matriarchs who do not submit to the will of their men. In actuality most black women have been more than willing to surrender control over their hard-earned resources to the men in their lives: fathers, brothers, lovers, and husbands. No wonder, then, that at the very onset of the feminist movement when national surveys were conducted to determine how groups of men felt about women working, black men were always more accepting and supportive of women working outside the home than other groups. This was not an indication of black males being less sexist; rather, it was an affirmation that black males did not feel that they lost power when black women worked. Indeed, as gender equality in the workforce has become a norm, it is evident that men of all groups are less concerned about women working outside the home if they are able to control the finances. Even when a woman is wealthy, the man she mates with will not be put off by her greater economic resources if he is able to control them. Moreover, now that masses of women work outside the home, studies show that this has not brought about gender equality inside the home.

While critics of black male-and-female relationships are correct when they call attention to intense levels of conflict, they tend to misunderstand the nature of that conflict. Most black women and men are not fighting because women want gender equality and men want male dominance. More often than not they are fighting because one party feels the other party has failed to fulfill the role they agreed to play. Usually, males are the ones who renege. And their way out of the social contract is usually betrayal. They use and abuse. They abandon. In the eyes of patriarchal black woman they fail to deliver the goods. She responds to his failure with her own scripted version of contempt hoping she can goad him, nag him, change him, turn him into the man she wants him to be. To a grave extent patriarchal black males and females are frozen in time, trapped in a state of arrested development. Usually it is simply assumed that black women who head households, who go to work and take care of families, are more together than their black male counterparts who are not doing their part (not showing up, not playing child support). Yet the truth is more complex. Oftentimes black women who assume responsibility for the material survival of their families are as emotionally underdeveloped as the black men they label irresponsible. Just as patriarchal men who provide for families often publicly represent themselves as cool, calm, and collected, then privately show themselves to be a psychological mess, this is often the case with black women.

The relationships between patriarchal black males and females will be better understood when it is no longer tacitly assumed that she is emotionally stable and he is emotionally unstable. By considering the possibility that many black males *and* females are in a state of arrested development, trapped by fantasy bonding and allegiance to the false selves, we cannot only understand better the nature of conflict between us, we can begin to heal our wounds. We can begin to do the work of relational recovery. That work must start with breaking through the denial created by allegiance to sexism that teaches us to despise our need for emotional connections. This denial has been especially damaging to black males as sexism has allowed females the freedom to acknowledge and feel emotions even as we are devalued because of this. Therapist Terrence Real explains: "We force our children out of the wholeness and connectedness in which they begin their lives. Instead of cultivating intimacy . . . we teach boys and girls, in complementary ways, to bury their deepest selves, to stop speaking, or attending to, the truth, to hold in mistrust, or even in disdain, the state of closeness we all, by our natures, most crave. We live in an antirelational, vulnerability-despising culture, one that not only fails to nurture the skills of connection but actively fears them." As black people in a white-supremacist culture we have had a psychohistory of learning to utterly hide or repress our vulnerability in order to survive.

When this survival strategy links with the overall cultural devaluation of vulnerability it makes sense that so many black folks have wrongly interpreted invulnerability as a sign of emotional strength. Maintaining this survival strategy when we no longer have to fear extreme violence at the hands of racist whites has damaged our emotional and intimate bonds. The inability to be vulnerable means that we are unable to feel. If we cannot feel we cannot truly emotionally connect with one another. We cannot know love. No wonder then that the lovelessness that abounds in our culture is even more intense among African-Americans. Real shares the crucial insight that "men and women will not completely love one another until both recover the state of integrity in which they began their lives." This is the work black males and females must do if we are to build positive bonds in all areas of relationships to one another, not just in romantic bonds.

Cultivating relational skills has been difficult for many progressive black folks because to do so often places us in a relationship of conflict with our source figures. In many of our families obedience and corporal punishment were and are valued as positive signs of parental discipline. My parents become enraged when I identify their physical disciplining of me as abusive; they see it as the positive parenting that helped me become a success. They do not want to hear about the feelings of worthlessness, the suicidal urges, that dominated my teen years. They want to forget their verbal abuse. Or they want to downplay its negative impact. Their response is a common reaction from black people when parental abuse of children is the topic.

Rather than acknowledge the dysfunctional nature of our families, most black folks idealize their family of origins. (How many times do you hear a black celebrity—an entertainer or athlete—thanking god and family, particularly mothers?) Oftentimes the black parents who are being thanked have been harsh disciplinarians; more often than not the mothers have been domineering and possessive, especially toward their sons and shaming of their daughters. To defend ourselves against the reality that our parents were often a mixed bag of affirming support on some occasions and shaming on the other, we tend to focus solely on the good. Many of us were goaded by verbal abuse to achieve and suffer from inner feelings of worthlessness and inadequacy despite our successes. The internalized voice of the family may still be telling us "you will never amount to anything" and "you are crazy" or "you may fool other folks but you can't fool me." John Bradshaw defines the fantasy bond as "the illusion of connectedness we create with our major caretaker whenever our emotional needs are not adequately met." Often when adult black folks recall childhood memories they idealize the past and their parents. Bradshaw states: "The more emotionally deprived a person has been, the stronger his fantasy bond. And paradoxical as it sounds, the more a person has been abandoned, the more he tends to cling to and idealize his family and his parents. Idealizing parents means to idealize the way they raised you." Black males are much more likely than black females to idealize their mothers. This is the consequence of having been overindulged by doting moms whose sons "could do no wrong." Rarely do black mothers overindulge their daughters.

In many black families maternal adoration of sons leads to inappropriate bonding, to overt and covert emotional abuse. When a mother has sacrificed everything for her son, she usually sends him the message that he owes her, that he can never repay her (hence he is made to feel inadequate or that she should be his intimate relationship). He may feel he is betraying his mother by desiring a peer partnership.

Dysfunctional single mothers and abused married women who have intense rage toward the men who have abandoned them often use male children to meet their emotional needs; this is emotional sexual abuse. In some cases the mother may be lavishing affection on her son while also being verbally abusive about adult black males. She may say that "all men are dogs," that they are no "good," or that their penises should be "cut off." This teaches the boy fear and mistrust of adult men. It makes him fear becoming an adult man and as a consequence he may try to emotionally remain a boy forever. Dan Kiley labels this "the Peter Pan syndrome," which was the title of his best-selling book published in the late eighties.

In the chapter "Irresponsibility" Kiley asks, "Could manhood be that bad?" a question a boy asked after hearing negative attitudes about adult manhood. Kiley explains: "If you heard a horror story about growing up, wouldn't you consider staying right where you were? All you'd have to do is concentrate on being a child. . . . You'd have to play all the time, have fun no matter what happened, and pretend that reality was a job. . . . Irresponsibility is a key to staying young." More than any other group of male children in this nation black boys hear stories about adult black maleness that would fill any child with dread. Watching television he sees that black males are most often the bad guys, and whether bad or good they are the guys who die young. No wonder than that many young black males feel there is no reward in growing up and assuming responsibility. Usually, it is doting mothers—then, later on, doting girlfriends and wives—who enable this lack of self-development. Women who refuse to enable the black male Peter Pan become the targets for his repressed rage.

While some black males are overindulged by mothers in ways that disempower them, that keep them in a state of arrested development, most black males suffer more extreme forms of emotional abuse. They are the boys who are belittled, humiliated, shamed. They are the objects of unrelenting parental sadism. Maternal sadism expresses itself via constant complaint and rage-oholism. This is especially the case with mothers who are enraged that men in their lives are not doing their part. They may let the boy believe that he is the reason she is not free. Mothers may communicate their extreme worry over finances inadvertently or directly blame the child. She may make the child feel guilty that she has to spend her frugal salary on his upkeep. She may begrudge him small pleasures. Black male children abused in this way usually idealize their mothers, seeing them as "victims." Their goal in life is often to be successful so that they can provide for their mother. Yet their mother may be the person who constantly told them they were bad or destined to be a failure even as she expressed affection. Bradshaw points out that calling children "bad throughout their first seven years is abusive and does damage to their self-worth" and "spanking and punishing them for being bad causes them shame." The black male child who is shamed feels flawed and defective. Those feelings are no doubt compounded as he receives the message from mainstream culture that black men are monsters.

Like every violated and/or abused child, black boys may obey their mothers and fathers. As adult men they may praise their parents for giving them needed harsh discipline. However, deep down they may feel a fundamental need to get away from domineering mothers (and sometimes fathers) whom they may experience as engulfing, and they may have tremendous rage about their unmet emotional needs. And if incest, physical abuse, and addiction were part of the familial experience, a black male child (like his female counterpart) will be dysfunctional if there has been no positive intervention. Dysfunctional children become dysfunctional adults if they do not get help.

Black males who have suffered in this way are wounded adult children. They are daily the victims of toxic shaming.

Bradshaw describes the way internalized shame wounds the spirits: "Shame results from all forms of abandonment. Actual physical abandonment is shaming. . . . All forms of psychological abuse are shaming: yelling, belittling, name-calling, labeling, criticizing, judging, ridiculing, humiliating, comparing, contempting are all sources of shame. Shame-based parents are models of shame. How could shame-based parents possibly teach their children self-love?" Wounded children learn to skillfully cover up their shame. They wear the mask.

It should come as no surprise then that when these wounded men enter romantic bonds, problems arise. As the saying goes, "hurt people hurt people." Given the reality that damaged boys so often grow up to become men who choose partners who either mirror the parents who victimized them or assume the role of offender with a partner who in no way resembles their source figures, it makes sense that romantic bonds between black males and females overall remain fraught with conflict. Both the male and the female bring to their bonding unresolved pain. And they are both psychologically poised to act out. Black women may act out by being controlling (thus mirroring the domineering mother). They may deploy all the strategies of shaming, thus reenacting familiar patterns of abuse. Naturally, the wounded black male will respond with rage. Locked in patterns of codependency, they reinforce their wounds, they are unable to create love because to do so they would have to grow up. To achieve emotional maturity they would have to deal with the pain of the past.

Just as many black males are bringing to relationships a wounded inner child angry at his mother for not giving sustained connection, black females bring their wounded selves, their rage at fathers who have abandoned them. Black male-and-female romantic bondings have become more violent and rage-filled because violation in source relationships has become more common. When I was growing up my mother did not work during our formative years. And she was often the peacemaker, standing between us and Dad's abuse. She worked hard to create a peaceful caring home. And yet she was also sometimes domineering and verbally abusive. Traumatic abuse was occasionally inflicted by our raging violent dad. Luckily for us the good outweighed the bad. In most homes where parents are overworked, underpaid, and stressed out, there is no one present to do the work of peacemaking and emotional caregiving. This is one reason families become dysfunctional. When the struggle to survive converges with the world of addiction, then home becomes a living hell and everyone suffers. Yet even in black families where there is class privilege and material abundance, parents can be so immersed in working that they do not tend to the emotional well-being of children. They may believe that buying things and satisfying every material whim is all that is needed. Emotional neglect and abuse cuts across class and circumstance.

Relationships between black males and females will change for the good as more and more black folks become aware of the detrimental impact of patriarchal thinking and fundamentalist religious beliefs. Reclaiming the importance of emotional connection is crucial if we are to experience relational recovery. In *Creating Love* John Bradshaw writes: "One way to understand what constitutes functionality in a family is by dividing the word response-ability. Being able to respond is an ability. Functional families are created by functional people. Functional people have the ability to respond to each other's feelings, needs, thought, and wants. In functional families, all members are allowed to express what they feel, think, need, or want. Problems are dealt with openly and effectively." Clearly, to heal wounds created in dysfunctional bonds, black males and females must be committed to telling the truth, to practicing integrity.

Since betrayal is one of the primary causes of heartache between black males and females, commitment to honest and open communication is essential to making amends and creating love. M. Scott Peck calls this discipline "dedication to truth" and it must be continually employed "if our lives are to be

healthy and our spirits are to grow." In *The Road Less Traveled*
Peck states that "clinging to an outmoded view of reality is the
basis of much mental illness." African-Americans cultivated
many survival strategies that were needed when confronting
the brutal racist terrorism of state-sanctioned apartheid. One of
those strategies was the art of dissimulation, taking on any
appearance, identified in the vernacular as "wearing a mask." In
the terroristic circumstance the ability to mask feelings, to lie
and pretend, as well as the appearance of invulnerability, was
needed. Yet these outmoded survival strategies have been
detrimental in our intimate lives. And they are no longer useful
in the world outside the home. Black folks have been much
more willing to let them go in the outside world while still
clinging to them in intimate relationships.

Black men, like other groups of men in patriarchal culture,
have found that lying and withholding truth is a form of power.
Dominators use it to exploit and oppress others. Far too many
black men are addicted to lying. This addiction may have begun
in childhood as way to avoid harsh punishment or as a way to
keep from hurting overworked and tired parents. Yet it keeps
black males from knowing love. To be without integrity is to be
without the self-esteem that is the core of self-love. If a black
male does not love himself he will be unable to create a loving
relationship with anyone. And his romantic bonds will be
fraught with acting-out behavior. In many African-American
communities the black man who womanizes, whose whole life
is based on lies, secrets, and silences, is often seen as the epitome of desirable manhood. That's because patriarchal sex education teaches men that fucking is all that matters. So the womanizing man fucks a lot but rarely does he find fulfillment. In
part this was the message of the film *Sweet Sweetback's
Baadasssss Song*. The black "loverman" is always a man on the
run. He had no meaningful ties, no real home, no purpose. This
is another false self that dysfunctional black folks have tried to
represent as an image of power.

The designation of a black male as a "player" is really a euphemism for con artist. And while the player as pimp and hustler has been glamorized in diverse black communities, the truth is ultimately that he is a lonely man, running from himself. Often the sexually abused boy becomes the womanizer, the playboy. His sexual addiction is a way to avoid feelings. In *Heart of the Soul* Gary Zukav and Linda Francis describe it as "a defense against awareness of the most painful experience . . . the experience of being powerless." Addictive sexual behavior is a barrier to intimacy. When black males and females are exploiting one another, intimacy is not possible. Importantly Zukav and Frances state that "connecting the experience of addictive sexual attraction with the avoidance of painful emotions is a significant step in healing an addiction to sex." As black males and females cultivate emotional awareness, relational recovery will no longer seem impossible. Therapist Terrence Real writes in *How Can I Get Through to You?*: "The way to keep passion alive is by telling the truth—the truth about what we see, what we feel, what we really want. . . . Mature love requires us to acknowledge our full experience, our feelings and wants, while making grown-up choices about them." To heal the hurt between black males and females we have to learn to dialogue, to do active listening.

Working with couples to restore their relationships Terrence Real encourages them to learn to communicate and negotiate. He states: "Relational esteem helps us understand how to speak the truth to ourselves. Learning to speak rationally provides a map for telling our truth to others. In order to live beyond patriarchy we must allow ourselves to drop each day to levels of vulnerability." Many black males are longing to be given permission to be vulnerable, hoping that female relatives, friends, lovers, will assure them that they gain personal power by opening the heart, by choosing the experience of intimacy over hardheartedness. Offering a helpful strategy to couples seeking reconciliation Real encourages us to scan for the positive, which he says means "sifting through what you hear for those things you can agree to and give." With compassion and keen, brilliant insight he shares that men often see scanning for the positive as an act of submission: "One frequently hears that men are frightened of intimacy. I don't believe that is true. I think that many men don't know what intimacy is. The one-up, one-down world of masculinity leaves little space for tenderness. One is either controlled of controlling, dominator or dominated. When men speak of fearing intimacy what they really mean is that they fear subjugation. In a visceral way, most men in our culture experience vulnerability as opening themselves up to be overrun." Given the long history of enforced subordination that black males have endured as a consequence of racist exploitation and oppression, added to patriarchy's equation of vulnerability with castration, the fear of being subjugated is intensified for black men. Because many black women who are not emotionally mature are often controlling, it is all the more threatening for black men to open up, be emotionally receptive, and listen. Yet this is the work that needs to be done. Courageous black males and females are doing the work of love.

I am such a fix-it person, which means that I often err on the side of being controlling or at least appearing that way. Since I am a person who talks and my partner is more the silent type it is helpful for us to have a short weekly meeting where we take turns facilitating and talking in a equal manner. Since he, like many men, is more comfortable in the space of a "meeting" and is confident that he knows how to conduct himself, we both are afforded the opportunity to engage in negotiations, to move from complaint to request, to make reasonable demands, or comfortable invitations. In the relationships I have with black males I am fortunate to know men who are willing to process, to come together at the table of love and do the work of relational recovery.

Years ago, I was talking with a black woman friend about my longing for a relationship and she kept pressing me to tell what

I wanted. And when I calmly stated: "I want a partner who is willing to process, to dialogue, and negotiate." She laughed and replied, "You don't want a black male then." Leaving this conversation I then articulated the same longing with a black male philosopher, who echoed her sentiments, saying "Black men do not want to be existentially self-reflective," which is to say that they do want to be self-determining agents responsible for their choices in relationships.

While these sentiments are no doubt an accurate account of where many black men stand, it is as true to state that black men are longing for love and since that longing cannot be satisfied until they do recovery work, individual black men are eager to feel and heal, to process. Writer Kevin Powell is doing the work of processing when in his essay "Confessions of a Recovering Misogynist" he says: "Just as I feel it is whites who need to be more vociferous about racism in their communities, I feel it is men who need to speak long and loud about sexism among each other. . . . The fact is there was a blueprint handed to me in childhood telling me this is the way a man should behave, and I unwittingly followed the script verbatim. There was no blueprint handed to me about how to begin to wind myself out of sexism as an adult. . . . Everyday I struggle with myself." As black males and females struggle with ourselves, doing the internal recovery work, we come to our relationships prepared, ready to do the work of love. Relational recovery began for African-Americans the moment slavery ended. Like the myth of Isis traveling around the world to find the dismembered parts of her beloved brother Osiris so that she can help him be whole again, black males and females have a long and fruitful legacy to draw on, life maps that chart our searching for the ways to come together and stay together in love. Our task is to learn to read and follow those maps.

Relational recovery will lead black males and females away from the dominator model of relationships, where one person is up and the other person down. It will lead us away from patriarchy toward a loving feminist politics that will enable us to fully embrace gender equality. And, more importantly, to sustain a vision of loving relationships rooted in mutuality, a vision that says there is enough love for all of us, our needs can be met and our longings fulfilled. This is the love Toni Morrison evokes in her eighties' novel *Beloved* when she creates an image of the black male as healer of wounded hearts, able to "take the broken bits and pieces that I am and give them back to me in the right order." In the sixties, working in therapy to recover myself, I wrote long passages about my grandfather, a loving black male, which were later included in the autobiography of my childhood *Bone Black*. I declared: "His smells fill my nostrils with the scent of happiness. With him the broken bits and pieces of my heart come together again." These visions of black men as healers, able to nurture life, are the representations of black masculinity that "keep it real" for they offer the vision of what is possible, a hint of the spirit that is alive and well in the black male collective being, ready to be reborn. They take our minds and hearts away from images of black males who have known soul murder and speak to us of resurrection, of a world in the making where all is well with black men's souls, where they are free and made whole.

Chapter 9

healing the hurt

Teaching classes on race and gender I often stand at the front of classrooms looking out at a diverse body of students who are more often than not eager to tell me that racism and sexism are no longer a problem, that differences do not really matter, that no one notices because "we are all just people." Then the next time we meet I ask them if they were able to die and be born again, which racialized body they would choose and why: a white male, a white female, a black male, or a black female. No matter the make-up of the class—sometimes predominantly white, and other times predominantly black and/or people of color, sometimes mostly female and sometimes a fifty-fifty split between female and males—overwhelmingly folks want to come back as white and male. The reasons they give all confirm the race/sex hierarchy in our nation; they all simply believe they will have a better chance at success and at living long and well if they are white males. The number of response for each category usually follows the lines of the existing social order: white male, white female, black male, black female. Usually no one, even black females, chooses to return as a black female.

No matter the amount of information students have received from mass media about black men being an endangered species, they look around and see that when it comes to fame and fortune individual privileged black men do better than black women. Even though black females may have access to more jobs than black males, better education, a higher life expectancy, lower likelihood of being imprisoned, everyone understands that if you look from the top down rather than from the bottom up, male privilege gives black males reaching the top far more than it does black females. Of course the reality is that far more black men hit bottom than reach the top.

By writing this book I hoped to challenge the misguided notion that ours is a culture that loves black men. I wanted to make it clear that there is a crisis in the black male spirit in our nation. And that crisis is not because black men are an "endangered species"; rather, it is a crisis perpetuated by widespread dehumanization, by the continued placement of black males outside the category of human, one that identifies them as animal, beast, other—which is precisely what happens when anyone deploys the phrase most commonly used to speak of animals, *endangered species*, when describing the lot of black men. It is worthy to note that unenlightened white folks began to use this phrase as more black female voices swelled in challenging black male sexism and calling on black folks to stop sexism and male domination in black life.

Wise progressive black women have understood for some time now that the most genocidal threat to black life in America, and especially to black male life, is patriarchal thinking and practice. Wise progressive black women have understood that any coming together of free, whole, decolonized black males and females would constitute a formidable challenge to imperialist white-supremacist capitalist patriarchy.

Historically and today, white-supremacist patriarchy has found that the best way to prevent solidarity between black females and males is to make it appear that females are getting power while black male power is diminishing. It is the old "man, she's got you pussy whipped" strategy of divide and conquer once again. And as in the past it works.

Any student of black liberation can tell you that slavery ended and civil rights became a reality for black people in this country in part because of the joint participation of black males and females in resistance struggle. It has served the interests of all who are the enemies of black self-determination to keep black females and males vying for the position of most oppressed, rather than working together to end our collective suffering. When the issue is suffering, the truth of our lives as African-Americans is best understood by the simple phrase "hurt people hurt people." We are all suffering. When black males are in pain we are all in pain.

If there is any distinction to be made between the status of black females and males it does not lie with a difference in the substantive nature of suffering or in the degree of life-threatening risk. What is different for black males, what makes it harder for them to survive than black females, is the dearth of healing theory and practice addressing black male pain and possibility (which includes support networks and therapeutic interventions), as well as the collective refusal on the part of black males to constructively use the resources that are available for their empowerment. While most black males and females buy into toxic patriarchal thinking, usually black females survive by being flexible and breaking with patriarchal thinking when necessary. For example, my father never wanted Mama to work, but she understood that to ensure the educational advancement of her children she needed to bring money in. She defied him to go out and work. Working helped her self-esteem. She moved positively forward and helped us all move forward, and Dad stayed stuck, pissed that she went out to work. His rage at her defiance created negativity and conflict, diminishing the well-being of both of them and of the family as a whole. Rigid rules, support of male dominance in decision-making even when it is wrongminded, are both part of patriarchal thinking.

Naming the rules of patriarchy in *Creating Love* John Bradshaw cites these four: the insistence on blind obedience; the repression of all emotions, except fear; the destruction of individual willpower; and the repression of thinking whenever it departs from the viewpoints of authority figures. In today's world black boys are socialized into patriarchal thinking just as systematically as my father's generation was decades ago. Kevin Powell describes the process in his essay "Confession of a Recovering Misogynist": "I am a sexist male. . . . It is not that I was born this way—rather I was born into this male-dominated society, and consequently, from the very moment I began forming thoughts, they formed in a decidedly male-centered way. . . . My mother, working-poor and a product of the conservative and patriarchal South, simply raised me as most women are taught to raise boys: the world was mine; there were no chores to speak of, and my aggressions were considered normal, something that we boys carry out as a rite of passage." It was only when he saw himself acting violently toward females he cared about that Powell began the process of learning anti-sexist thinking; that thinking has been life-saving and life-enhancing for him. His transformation shows that change is possible, that black men who choose to do so can learn new ways of thinking and new habits of being.

Few black men can look at the data about black male lives and not see clearly the dangers they face and the extent to which those dangers are in place because of their blind allegiance to dominator culture. Black male–on–black male homicide would not exist if it were not encouraged and reinforced by notions of patriarchal manhood and white supremacy. For if it was just about manhood shootouts, black males would be killing white men at the same rates that they kill one another. They buy into the racist/sexist assumption that the black male is valueless and therefore when you take a black man's life you are just taking nothing from nothing, This is as nihilism lived. In the essay "It's Raining Men" Robert F. Reid-Pharr describes black men as the most "unfree of American citizen" stating these facts: "As one-third of the black males in this country languish in prisons or under the stewardship of assorted probation and parole boards, as black men continue to be over represented in the drug trade, and among the legions of persons with chronic illnesses—HIV, cancer, heart disease, alcoholism; as we give our lives over to violence or to a certain silent despair, we have become the emblem of ugliness, bestiality, and barbarism." The imperialist white-supremacist capitalist patriarchal society we are living in is to blame for much of the horrors black men must face. However, black males are responsible for the manner in which they confront those horrors or fail to do so. Black males then must be held accountable when they betray themselves, when they choose self-destructive paths.

Most black men are clinging to outmoded survival strategies, of which patriarchal thinking is one, because they fear that if they give up what little "power" they may have in the existing system they will have nothing. This is an irrational fear but it has such a chokehold on the black male psyche because of the soul murder that takes places in childhood. It is that soul murder that Richard Wright describes when he writes, "They don't let you feel what you want to feel." In John Bradshaw's book *Bradshaw On: The Family* he states: "Soul-murder is the basic problem in the world today; it is the crisis in the family. We programmatically deny children their feelings. . . . Once a person loses contact with his own feelings, he loses contact with his own body. . . . To have one's feelings, body, desires and thoughts controlled is to lose one's self. To lose one's self is to have one's soul murdered." Unlike black females, who are given permission by sexist thinking to be emotional and therefore able to remain in touch with our feelings in childhood even when we are abused or taught to mask them to appear "strong," black males are required by rituals of patriarchal manhood to surrender their capacity to feel. The soul-murdered black boy then has a much harder time recovering himself than the damaged girl has. Tragically, the patriarchal thinking the black man embraces is precisely the logic that will keep him mentally enslaved and mentally ill. Enlightened black men know this. This is why the mission statement of the group Black Men for the Eradication of Racism clearly states: "We've accepted a definition of ourselves that's killing us in a way no bullet ever could."

While most black women do not identify with anti-patriarchal thinking or support feminism, they, like other groups of women, benefit from the feminist focus on healing. The feminist movement successfully put in place a politics of self-recovery and self-help that directly addresses female pain and offers strategies for transformation. A significant body of work by progressive black women has emerged which prioritizes healing. In a postscript to the essay "A Phenomenology of the Black Body" black writer Charles Johnson offers the valuable insight that in an "amazing and revolutionary feat of cultural reconstruction, contemporary black women have made dominant the profile of the female body as first and foremost spiritual." Collectively black males have yet to intervene on the negative cultural representations of the black male body because they simply cannot change how they are seen (as brutes, beasts, bastards) without challenging patriarchal notions of manhood as well as white-supremacist notions of black male identity.

Black males can engage and learn from healthy self-loving black women strategies of self-recovery. The progressive writing that has challenged existing stereotypes and offered black females alternative ways to see ourselves was never written solely for a female audience. Yet to glean healing wisdom from the work of black female writers, black males do need to practice empathy. Significantly, just as visionary black females began to produce a body of liberation literature that aids us all in the process of self-recovery and self-determination, we began to hear about the dearth of black leaders. We began to be told via mass media (usually with sexist black males as the mouthpieces) that black females could not raise a healthy black male child. Added to this was the mass-media–driven patriarchal Million Man March, which promoted sexist gender norms and whose rhetoric simply echoed Daniel Patrick Moynihan's 1965 report "The Negro Family: The Case for National Action." All of these attacks on progressive anti-patriarchal movements in black life have happened courtesy of white patriarchy. Yet unaware black males get seduced by patriarchy—The Man— again and again no matter how much it violates them and keeps them down. Patriarchal black women are part of the problem. They reenact the shame-based dramas that wound black male spirit. As Quinn Eli shares in his autobiographical essay, "A Liar in Love," black females were often the people who put his masculinity in check via rituals of humiliation. He confesses: "A woman I knew had a way of convincing the men in her life that her unhappiness was somehow their fault—and that this inability to make her happy was related in some way to their masculinity. . . . So in my fights with her for dominance and control, she was almost always the victor, because as soon as she felt threatened enough she'd invariably call out, 'You don't know shit about being a man.' And, like a balloon stabbed abruptly with the tip of a pin, I would burst and then sputter to the ground." The kind of humiliation he suffered at the hands of a patriarchal black woman is a common occurrence—one that begins for many black males in childhood with mothers who begin to let their sons know that they have failed as "men" before they can barely walk. Even as an adult man Kevin Powell still fears his mother's ability to take him down. He writes: "There are days when speaking with her turns me back into that little boy, cowering beneath the belt and tongue of a woman deeply wounded by my father, by poverty, by the sexism that dominated her life." Given this history of material sadism, so often manifested in black male life as shaming about manhood, it is no wonder that many black males fear black females, seeing us always and only as controlling domineering bitches that they cannot listen to.

When visionary black women bring a healing message that could empower black males they get the red alert warning from all the Big Daddy patriarchal inner voices lurking within: he should not listen to anything she has to say, she is just trying to bring him down. Aware black men who do listen, like the group of brothers who work at Men Stopping Violence, find their inner voices silenced. These anti-sexist black men wrote to Minister Farrakhan and others to critique the sexism of the Million Man March, stating up front, "We are black men who are working to end all male violence against women" and concluded by urging the organizers "to consider the physical, mental, and spiritual consequences of reinforcing the notion that Black men intend to 'take over' the leadership of families" but no mass media turned the spotlight in their direction.

One of the fundamental handicaps progressive anti-sexist black males face is that they have no national platform from which to educate for critical consciousness. The feminist movement, along with woman-centered self-help, not only led to the formation of platforms women of all races used to spread the word. It also showed that women were willing to pay for products advancing the cause of self-recovery, creating a new market. No famous charismatic anti-sexist black male leaders seeking to educate black men for critical consciousness have come to power on a platform for saving the souls of black men, for helping black men address their problems by first and foremost engaging in the practice of self-love.

Individual black males searching for new life strategies utilize in a productive way the visionary work of black women. They embrace enlightened black women as teachers and comrades. Listening to healthy emotionally mature black females is essential to black male self-recovery. In interviews with recovering black males I asked them to name life strategies they utilized for self-empowerment and a large majority of them cited seeking help from black females. In diverse black communities sexism has often led folks to assume that the leader, healer, or spiritual teacher needs to be a black male. Shortly before he was assassinated Malcolm X praised black women for our contribution in the struggle for freedom: "I'm one person who's for giving them all the leeway possible because they've made a greater contribution than many of us men." Listening to and learning from progressive black women is one way for black men to begin the work of self-recovery.

Black men need not prolong their pain while engaging in savior searching—that is, waiting for the black male leader who will rescue them. In *The Heart of the Soul*, Gary Zukav and Linda Francis define savior searching as "the effort to locate an individual or circumstance that can deliver you from your discomfort." They warn that savior searching can take the mundane form of believing you will be transformed by money, fame, education, a perfect mate, job, or automobile. I call this living on the principle of "if only." Many black males sit around believing they could it get together "if only." The only way to salvation is for black men to look within, to recognize themselves as the source of their well-being.

In *Rock My Soul: Black People and Self-Esteem* I suggest that in today's world "mental health is the revolutionary frontier for black people." Sound mental health begins with self-esteem. Many black males, even those who have all the outer trappings of success, feel low self-esteem. In *Six Pillars of Self-Esteem* Nathaniel Branden states: "Self-esteem, fully realized, is the experience that we are appropriate to life and to the requirements of life—self-esteem is the confidence in our ability to think, confidence in our ability to cope with the basic challenges of life, and confidence in our right to be successful and happy, the feelings of being worthy, deserving, entitled to assert our needs and wants, achieve our values and enjoy the fruits of our efforts." The six pillars of self-esteem are personal integrity, self-acceptance, self-responsibility, self-assertion, living consciously, and living purposefully. In *Rock My Soul* I write about the ways individuals lacking in self-esteem lose their sense of agency: "They feel powerless. They feel they can only be victims." This sense of always and only being a victim is one of the factors preventing wounded black males from reclaiming a lost sense of agency. Since that loss of agency, which is also an aftermath of soul murder, may be a consequence of childhood trauma more than the result of a vicious encounter with racism, then the healing process must begin with confronting the past or at least living differently from it in order to live fully in the present.

To build the self-esteem that is the foundation of self-love black males necessarily engage in a process of resistance, during which they challenge existing negative stereotypes and reclaim their right to self-definition. To achieve that end they must do spiritual work. I use the word *spiritual* here, not in the sense of organized ritual but in the more metaphysical sense of cultivating care of the soul. Just as Charles Johnson identified contemporary black female insistence on the primacy of our spiritual beingness as a counter to the racist/sexist dehumanization that would see us as always and only depraved bodies, black males must cultivate a language of heart and soul.

Visionary black males like Joseph Beam, Essex Hemphill, Marlon Riggs, and Kevin Powell began to fashion this language in essays, poetry, and filmmaking. Three of these men, all gay, have died young. Their gayness in and of itself did not make them more "aware." There are many gay men who are just as stuck and psychologically messed up as their straight counterparts. Beam, Hemphill, and Riggs were all men who chose to move themselves from self-hate to self-love. They did the work of love. It was not easy.

Joseph Beam began his introduction to *In the Life*, the

anthology of black gay male writers he edited with an homage to black gay women writers (Audre Lorde, Barbara Smith, June Jordan, Michelle Cliff), stating: "Their courage told me that I, too, could be courageous. I, too, could not only live with what I feel, but could draw succor from it, nurture it, and make it visible." As his consciousness developed about the primacy of creating self-love he shares these realizations. He explores the way black males relate to one another, starting with his dad. Beam writes: "How difficult it is to speak of my appreciation saying: Dad, I love you. . . . Our love for each other, though great, may never be spoken. It is the often unspoken love that Black men give to other Black men in a world where we are forced to cup our hands over our mouths or suffer under the lash of imprisonment, unemployment, or even death. But these words, which fail, are precisely the words that are life-giving and continuing. They must be given voice. What legacy is to be found in silence? Because of the silence among us, each one of us, as Black boys and men maturing, must all begin the struggle to survive anew." It is this cycle of damage that must be broken if black men are to be free and made whole.

Beam understood this, declaring:

I dare myself to dream of us moving from survival to potential, from merely getting by to a positive getting over. I dream of Black men loving and supporting other Black men, and relieving Black women from the role of primary nurturers in our community. I dream, too, that as we receive more of what we want from each other that our special anger reserved for Black women will disappear. I dare myself to dream. . . . I dare myself to dream of a time when I will pass a group of brothers on the corner, and the words 'fucking faggot' will not move the air around my ears, and when my gay brother approaches me on the street that we can embrace if we choose. I dare us to dream that we are worth wanting each other. Black men loving Black men is the revolutionary act.

Riggs, Hemphill, and I spent many hours debating this last statement. Black male friends and comrades, who gave me unconditional love free of judgment, whether baking me a cake for my birthday or telling my latest flame that they were watching him and were there to be a witness guarding my heart's treasure, they respected me as a thinker and an intellectual. So when I told them, "No way, honey—black men dealing with their childhoods is the revolutionary act," they got it. The lightbulbs went off. They understood that without self-recovery work black males would not find their way to the self-love that would allow them to love another. I miss their witness and the joy we shared.

In conversation, another comrade of ours, filmmaker Isaac Julien, told Hemphill that "unlearning self-hatred and fear is hard work." Knowing this intimately, he feels it is important for black males to claim their failure as a way to resist the perfectionism patriarchal manhood demands. Julien states: "I think failure is something that should be celebrated. I don't want to buy into a formation of black male identity where one has to hold oneself in a rigid way—as in a march—even against how we might feel about ourselves in terms of our pain, our skepticism, lack and self-doubt. All these things are as much a part of black male identity as the things we might want to parade, like toughness and unity. We have to be willing to engage in a process of thinking through our failure as black men in this society. . . . Black macho discourses of empowerment will never truly reach us where we live. There is something interesting we can learn from our so-called failure, because our failure also contains our resistance." Awakening the collective spirit of resistance in black males will be the revolutionary energy that will change the fate of black males. Until that moment comes, black males must, as Beam declared, "dare to dream."

They must dream about masculinity that humanizes, They must dare to embrace boyhood as a time of wonder, play, and self-invention. They must dare to become men who are willing to be different, who, as Olga Silverstein writes in *The Courage to Raise Good Men*, will be "empathic and strong, autonomous and connected, responsible to self, to family and friends, and to society, and capable of understanding how those responsibilities are, ultimately, inseparable." Kay Hagan reminds us that men who are different, who are anti-sexist, who are self-loving, "can be somewhat disturbing to be around because they usually do not act in ways associated with typical men." She explains further: "They listen more than they talk; they self-reflect on their behavior and motives; they actively educate themselves about women's reality by seeking out women's culture and listening to women. . . . They avoid using women for vicarious emotional expression. . . . When they err—and they do err— they look to women for guidance, and receive criticism with gratitude. They practice enduring uncertainty while waiting for a new way of being to reveal previously unconsidered alternatives to controlling and abusive behavior. They intervene in other men's misogynist behavior, even when women are not present, and they work hard to recognize and challenge their own . . . [they] perceive the value of a feminist practice for themselves and they advocate it not because it's politically correct, or because they want women to like them, or even because they want women to have equality, but because they understand that male privilege prevents them not only from becoming whole, authentic human beings but also from knowing the truth about the world. They continue to open the door." The doors of the soul have been closed for many black males. And it is as they unlock those doors and find the courage to enter that they discover themselves anew.

Chapter 10

the coolness of being real

Once upon a time black male "cool" was defined by the ways in which black men confronted the hardships of life without allowing their spirits to be ravaged. They took the pain of it and used it alchemically to turn the pain into gold. That burning process required high heat. Black male cool was defined by the ability to withstand the heat and remain centered. It was defined by black male willingness to confront reality, to face the truth, and bear it not by adopting a false pose of cool while feeding on fantasy; not by black male denial or by assuming a "poor me" victim identity. It was defined by individual black males daring to self-define rather than be defined by others.

Using their imaginations to transcend all the forms of oppression that would keep them from celebrating life, individual black males have created a context where they can be self-defining and transform a world beyond themselves. Critic Stanley Crouch attests to this power in the *All-American Skin*

Game, Or, the Decoy of Race when he writes about Louis
Armstrong: "Lifting his trumpet to a scarred embouchure, he
rose from the gumbo pot of the Western Hemisphere like a
brown Poseidon of melody. Armstrong was then calling up the
heroic, Afro-American lyricism of hope swelling out beyond
deep recognition of tragedy, and was also enriching our ambiva-
lent sense of adult romance through the beat of that matchless
dance in which all of the complexities of courtship and romantic failure seem to have located themselves in the Argentinian
steps of endless ballroom couples so expressive of passion
nuance they seem forever mythic. The transcending power of
such combinations is symbolic of the affirmative, miscegenated
heat necessary to melt down the iron suits of history." If every
young black male in America simply studied the history, the
life, and work of black musicians, they would have blueprints
for healing and survival. They would see clearly the roads they
can take that will lead to a life of suffering and pain and the
roads they can take that will lead to paradise, to healing, to a life
lived in community.

In the opening statement of his autobiography *Blues All
Around Me* B.B. King declares: "When it comes to my own life,
others may know the cold facts better than me. . . . Truth is, cold
facts don't tell the whole story. . . . I'm not writing a cold-
blooded history. I'm writing a memory of my heart. That's the
truth I'm after—following my feelings no matter where they
lead. I want to try to understand myself, hoping that you . . . will
understand me as well." In previous chapters I have talked
about the blues as a musical form black males once chose
because it allowed them to express a range of complex emotions,
from the most intense joy to profound heartbreak and sorrow.

Sharing what the blues meant to him as a boy King states:
"Blues meant hope, excitement, pure emotion. Blues were
about feelings." Just as today's gangsta rap invites black males to
adopt a cool pose, to front and fake it, to mask true feelings, the
blues was an invitation to black men to be vulnerable, to

express true feelings, to break open their hearts and expose them. Black males have helped create the blues, more than any other music, as a music of resistance to the patriarchal notion that a real man should never express genuine feelings. Emotional awareness of real-life pain in black men's lives was and is the heart and soul of the blues. When the guitar player sings, "I found a leak in my building, and my soul has got to move. I say my soul has got to move," he is singing about the pain of betrayal, about the soul's need not to be abandoned, to find shelter in a secure emotional place. He is giving lyric voice to all that Thomas Moore writes about in his best-selling book *Care of the Soul*.

Writing about the transformative power of the blues, Stanley Crouch offers this powerful insight: "The blues is the sound of spiritual investigation in a secular frame, and through its very lyricism, the blues achieves its spiritual penetration." Were masses of young blacks listening to the blues they would make the connection between, on the one hand, a serious politics of cool that is about recognizing the meaning of spiritual quest in a secular life where self-actualization requires an understanding, and, on the other, appreciation of the need to nurture the inner life of the spirit as a survival strategy. Any black male who dares to care for his inner life, for his soul, is already refusing to be a victim.

It is no accident that one of the moments of heartbreak in the career of B.B. King happened at a sixties concert where he confronted a world that was turning away from the blues. A new generation of black folks wanted to dance and swing, to party and do their thing—a generation that did not want to deal with the pain of the past or of the present. King remembers: "The sixties were filled with beautiful soul because black people were more vocal about the respect we wanted and the good feeling we had about ourselves. The politics seeped into the music, and the politics were about life-affirming change." Had these politics been truly liberating they would have embraced the blues as a powerful legacy of black male redemption. Instead, King recalls: "We want to get ahead. But in pushing ahead, sometimes we resent the old forms of music. They represent a time we'd rather forget, a period of history where we suffered shame and humiliation. Makes no difference that the blues is an expression of anger against shame or humiliation. In the minds of many young blacks the blues stood for a time and place they'd outgrown." This contempt for powerful legacies of black male identity in resistance set the stage for the hip-hop generation's disdain for the emotional complexity of black male experience.

Patriarchal hip-hop ushered in a world where black males could declare that they were "keeping it real" when what they were really doing was taking the dead patriarchal protest of the black power movement and rearticulating it in forms that, though entertaining, had for the most part no transformative power, no ability to intervene on politics of domination, and turn the real lives of black men around. While the patriarchal boys in the hip-hop crew may talk about keeping it real, there has been no musical culture with black men at the forefront of its creation that has been as steeped in the politics of fantasy and denial as the more popular strands of hip-hop. The fake cool pose of "keeping it real" has really meant covering up the fact that the generations of black folks dissing the blues and engaging in modern-day shoot-outs in which patriarchal hip-hop symbolically murders blues and by extension jazz, has really been an expression of dominator culture.

Todd Boyd explains the link between the black power movement and hip-hop culture in *The New H.N.I.C.* (his title embraces the rhetoric of dominator culture—it's all about the patriarchal vision of being on top, of being the ruler, of being Mr. Big, The Man). Boyd writes:

The Black Power movement, by contrast, was generally thwarted by the state at the mass level, but lingering tenets of this ideology have had a massive impact at the grassroots level. A conscious refusal to integrate with mainstream America now characterizes those Black people who willingly exist in their own world. Hip hop is an outgrowth of this black nationalist sentiment. . . . It is one thing to produce culture when people are legally barred from existing in the mainstream, but it is something else entirely for people to produce culture when integration appears to be an option and they choose, for whatever reasons, not to pursue it. Whereas Motown was packaged for mainstream consumption, hip hop was packaged by the sentiments of Black nationalism, and codified in the logo of the hip-hop fashion line FUBU, which means, "for us, by us."

This is the stuff of pure fantasy, since not only is hip-hop packaged for mainstream consumption, many of its primary themes—the embrace of capitalism, the support of patriarchal violence, the conservative approach to gender roles, the call to liberal individualism—all reflect the ruling values of imperialist white-supremacist capitalist patriarchy, albeit in black face. Just as the weak link in the militant black power movement was the obsession dysfunctional radical black males had with competition with white boys for patriarchal turf, hip-hop, especially gangsta rap, articulates this obsession in new forms but it's the same old song. Black men wanting to be "in charge"—in charge of the war, in charge of the woman, in charge of the world.

No wonder, then, most hip-hop culture offers black males very little "real" spiritual nourishment. Sure, it may teach them to play the dominator game and, sure, they may play all the way to wealth. But it does not teach them how to move beyond gaming to find the place of soulfulness, of being, of a cool that is about being well in your soul, being real.

Speaking of keeping it real, Boyd writes: "Hip hop is concerned on the other hand with being 'real,' honoring the truth of one's own convictions, while refusing to bend over to accommodate the dictates of the masses. Unlike the previous generation of people who often compromised or made do, in search of something bigger, hip-hop sees compromise as false, fake, and bogus." This version of being "real" sounds more like warmed-over versions of white patriarchal masculinity's notion that a real man proves his manhood by remaining rigidly attached to one's position, refusing to change. It reveals the emotional immaturity that underlies much hip-hop sentiment. Ironically the mature struggles for social justice, like civil rights, that made it possible for the hip-hop generation to bop their way forward without suffering significant racist assault and repression is mocked by Boyd, who unselfconsciously states: "In the same way that civil rights spoke to the conditions back in the day, hip hop artists now speak to a populace often disillusioned by those considered overtly political in a traditional sense." Much hip-hop culture is mainstream because it is just a black minstrel show—an imitation of dominator desire, not a rearticulation, not a radical alternative. No wonder, then, that patriarchal hip-hop culture has done little to save the lives of black males and done more to teach them, as Gwendolyn Brooks's prophetic poem which used the popular vernacular phrase "we real cool" as its title, states, to embrace a vision of "we real cool" that includes the assumption that "we die soon."

Boyd's definition of cool links it to the state of being lifeless, to necrophilia: "Cool is about a detached, removed, nonchalant sense of being. An aloofness that suggests one is above it all. A pride, an arrogance even, that is at once laid back, unconcerned, perceived to be highly sexual and potentially violent." This definition of black male cool rearticulates the way unenlightened white male hipsters read black masculinity. It is a fake stereotyped notion of cool, that denies the history of the "real cool," which was not about disassociation, hardheartedness, and violence, but rather about being intensely, connected, aware, and able to judge the right action to take in a given circumstance. Boyd's commonplace version of black male cool defines it in terms that mirror the traits of sociopaths and psychopaths;

it's all about disassociation. As such it is a vision of black masculinity that merely reinforces the status quo. It offers no pos-
sibilities of redemptive change or healing. It is the ultimate
drug that keeps black men addicted to the status quo and in
their place.

Though Boyd, and many of his cronies, like to think that
calling themselves "niggas" and basking in the glory of gangsta
culture, glamorizing addiction to drugs, pussy, and material
things, is liberation, they personify the spritual zombiehood of
today's "cool" black male. They have been bought with a price;
they are not their own. And the sad fact is that they do not even
know they are faking and fronting while mouthing off about
keeping it real; they bring new meaning to the word *denial*. In
actuality the culture they promote is all about playing dead and
loving it, or being dead and leaving behind a legacy of death.
Boyd gives expression to the deadness that is at the core of
patriarchal hip-hop's contempt for black history and culture
when he writes: "The civil rights movement was dour. It was
serious, and it was ultimately heavy in the way that it bore on
the soul. Many people, black, white, and otherwise, have
embraced this era while rejecting any subsequent era as failing
to live up to the standards of the one previous. . . . America has
now turned Martin Luther King Jr.'s dream into a long week-
end. In other words, civil rights has passed; get over it!" Boyd
seems to miss the point that nostalgia for the civil rights movement is linked to the humanizing blueprints for freedom that it
offered black folks, especially black males, upholding values
that were life-enhancing, that enabled many black males to
achieve healthy esteem without embracing dominator culture.

The black power movement with its faulty embrace of
gangsta culture and violence colluded with the dominant culture in producing a cult of death that is the current ethos of
black male life. Sure, individual black men are getting their
piece of the action, making money, making sex, making war, or
doing their own thing and maybe even having a good time, but

the fact remains that collectively black males today are in crisis, in a world of pain. And yeah! For many, death is the only way out. When hip-hop culture provides a blueprint for black male salvation we can value it as many of us value civil rights struggle. Hip-hop culture has created some fun subcultural playgrounds, some decent sounds and great grooves, but it has yet to "keep it real" by interfacing with the world beyond the subculture and mainstream commodification of blackness in a way that deadens to truly offer black males, young and old, blueprints for liberation, healing, a return to soul, wholeness.

Soul healing for wounded black males necessitates a return to the inner self. It requires that black males not only "come home" but that they dare to make of home a place where their souls can thrive. Mystic and spiritual teacher Howard Thurman was a black male of the blues generation. In seeking ecstatic union with the divine he found a way to be whole. Offering a strategy of healing in *Deep Is the Hunger*, Thurman tells us to bring a healing aesthetic to where we live, to create beauty. He writes: "To bring to the place where you live only the best and most beautiful, what a plan for one's life! This is well within the reach of everyone. Think of using one's memory in that way. As one lives from day to day, there are all sorts of experiences, good, bad, beautiful, ugly, that become a part of one's past. To develop the ability to screen one's memory so that only the excellent is retained for one's own room! All kinds of ideas pass through one's mind, about oneself, about the world, about people. Which do you keep for your own room? Think it over now, which ideas do you keep for the place where you live?" Creating beauty through art has been one of the most powerful ways individual black males have chosen to recover themselves, to declare their essential humanity. Whether it is the beauty of a Romare Bearden collage, a John Coltrane solo, or the exquisite photos of Roy DeCarava, individual black males have traditionally found a way to let their souls speak. And by that very act of speaking, of breaking silences, they resist dehumanization. John Coltrane's creates "A Love Supreme" after he chooses to do the work of recovery, turning away from the addiction that threatened to extinguish the creative spirit within him. Today's young black males seeking to find wholeness can find direction in the work and life of Coltrane, learning what not to do and what to do.

Coltrane took the broken bits and pieces of his heart and put them together again. His healing required that he assume accountability for driving away the life-threatening demons that led him to self-sabotage again and again. He was not afraid to face the truth of his life. Fear of facing the truth of their lives prevents most black males from finding themselves. As long as young black males believe that fronting, wearing the mask of "cool," is the thing to do when deep down a hot rage corrupts their spirit, black men will suffer. Every black male is diminished by the wanton destruction of black masculinity that is commonplace in our nation. Although Orlando Patterson has yet to embrace fully a critique of patriarchy he is one of the few black male scholars who has dared to speak the truth about the intense loneliness most black people, especially black males, feel in this culture.

Even though popular culture has made the black male body and presence stand for the apex of "cool," it is a death-dealing coolness, not one that is life-enhancing, for black males or the folks they associate with. Young males embrace a notion of cool that is about getting pussy and getting ready to kill (or a least to make somebody think you can kill) because as an identity this one is easier to come by than the quest to know the self and to create a life of meaning. Right now in our nation not enough adult black males chart the path to healthy self-esteem for younger black males. That path requires self-acceptance, assuming accountability, letting go the politics of blame, telling the truth, and being positive.

In the wake of the militant sixties, the patriarchal black power movement ushered in a politics of cool that was all about dominator culture, asserting power in the very ways righteous black men had criticized from the moment they touched earth in the so-called new world. This notion of cool was all about exploitation, the con, the hustle, getting over, getting by. Even though it dumped on the white man, it was all about being the white man, with all the perks and goodies that come with patriarchal dominator power. No wonder then that these black males had no respect for a notion of cool that was predicated upon black males' ability to use their prophetic imaginations to transcend the politics of domination and create beloved community. Patriarchal notions of cool have diminished the spirit of black male creativity. It has contained and in many cases crushed black male imagination.

Right now there is a generational divide between black males. Older black males often understand that embracing the cowboy masculinity of patriarchy dooms black men (they've seen the bodies fall down and not get up). They know cowboy culture makes black men kill or be killed, but younger black men are more seduced by the politics of being a gangsta, whether a gangsta academic or a gangsta rapper or a gangsta pimp. It is a seductive invitation to embrace death as the only logic of black male existence. In *Finding Freedom* Jarvis Jay Masters speaks to the reality that many black men seek prison, believing it to be their true destiny, their true home. He confesses: "Secretly we like it here. This place welcomes a man who is full of rage and violence. He is not abnormal here, not different. Prison life is an extension of his inner life." Refusing to accept a death sentence while still alive, Masters has found spiritual healing, a new life within prison walls. Importantly, he shares the path that led him to resurrection on death row: "When I first got charged with murder, it seemed unreal to me. . . . As other people started to do their job of finding a way to save my life, I joined the crusade. I had never cooperated before. But for the first time ever, I was determined to find out what was going on with me. I didn't want to justify the things I had done, and I wasn't cooperating now just to save my skin. Wanting to know the facts about myself made me take my life seriously for the first time." Masters offers black males a crucial insight into the healing process that begins when he makes the choice to take his life seriously.

When he began to critically reflect on the past, Masters remembered that it was the feeling of receiving a death sentence as a child, of hearing from the world around him that black boys did not matter, that sealed his fate. Opening his heart to spiritual healing through the practice of Buddhist meditation, Masters recovered his ability to wonder, to imagine. The fact that he can recover himself, even within the narrow confines of death row, should serve as a reminder to black males that salvation is always possible. It is always a question of choice.

Healthy black males in our society do not fall for the patriarchal hype. They attain emotional well-being by learning to love themselves and others. As responsible citizens they seek to do their part in the world of work, to be economically self-sufficient, but they do not believe money is the key to happiness. They cultivate a spiritual life, which may or may not include organized religion. In the memoir *Walking with the Wind*, civil rights activist and politician John Lewis speaks of the power of prayer in his life: "On the one hand prayer to me is an attempt to communicate with a power, with a force, with a being much greater than I am. On the other hand it is a period of simply having an executive session with yourself. It's a period of being alone, a period of meditation, a period of just being you." The key here is being, not doing.

Lewis continues: "When I look back on my own life and what I've come through, I can say that it was the prayers of the true believers, the prayers of an involved community of similar minds, that made it possible for me to still be here." For Lewis, prayer aids healing. He shares: "We can and do use it to deal with problems and the things and issues we don't understand, that we don't quite comprehend. It's very hard to separate the essence of prayer and faith. We pray because we believe that praying can make what we believe, our dreams and our vision, come true." Learning to pray, to meditate, to just be still is a practice that is healing. Although young black males often speak to believing in God, they often fail to take seriously a vision of God that is about loving and giving, rather than judgment and punishment. Moving away from the patriarchal god to a vision of cosmic divine spirit is one way that black males choose redemptive spiritual practices.

Black males who fully embrace the patriarchy will always be wedded to self-destructive behaviors, will always court death. To some extent every black male who has transgressed the boundaries set by racism and sexism has done so by repudiating some patriarchal rule. In his most recent book *Tough Notes: A Healing Call for Creating Exceptional Black Men* Haki Madhubuti states: "My brothers, there are exceptional men among us. Men who took their young years, most against great odds, to prepare themselves to be the best in their chosen field. Most of these men understood early how racism/white supremacy worked and therefore resisted its traps and temptations and fortified their bodies, minds, and spirits to rise against its evils." Just as he encourages black males to resist racism he encourages them to challenge sexist writing: "Gender equality, like human rights, is not modern paper talk, is not a reward given to smart women or good 'girls' but enlightened men. Gender quality is a hard fought right, earned by women and men who are not afraid of their own shadows, mistakes and histories." Black men who stand against sexism, who choose to be feminist in their thinking and action model a healing masculinity for all black men.

As black males turn away from patriarchal notions of coolness they will turn in the direction of a legacy of black male cool that remains life-enhancing, a legacy of grace. In *The Devil Finds Work* James Baldwin describes a religious rite called "pleading the blood":

When the sinner fell on his face before the altar, the soul of the sinner then found itself locked in battle with Satan: or, in the place of Jacob, wrestling with the angel. All of the forces of Hell rushed to claim the soul which has just been astonished by the light of the love of God. The soul in torment turned this way and that, yearning, equally for the light and the darkness: yearning, out of agony, for reconciliation—and for rest. . . . Only the saints who had passed through this fire had the power to intercede, to "plead the blood," to bring the embattled and mortally endangered soul "through." The pleading of the blood was a plea to whosoever had loved us enough to spill his blood for us, that he might sprinkle the soul with his love once more, to give us power over Satan, and the love and courage to live out our days.

Perhaps more than at any other point in our nation's history, black males today are caught in the psychological turmoil of longing equally for the light and the darkness. Now, more than ever before, the dark forces of addiction, of violence, of death, seem to have a more powerful grip on the black male soul than does the will to live, to love, to be healthy and whole. Now more than ever black males need those who love them enough to "plead the blood."

The black men I love most intimately share with me how hard it is for them to choose life over death, to choose to walk down the road that leads to paradise; it is so much easier to walk down the path of suffering and torment. To many black males this is a familiar prison without walls. It is a prison of their own making. Until we begin collectively to protect the emotional life of black boys and men we sign their death warrants. Saving the lives of black boys and black men requires of us all the courage to challenge patriarchal manhood, the courage to put in its place alternative visions of healing black masculinity.

I began this book telling the story of my brother and myself, partners in childhood until patriarchal violence separated us, wounding us in the place of our connectedness. When I look back, I see the joy and exuberance in my brother's face shutting down as he is forced to become the patriarchal performer, as he is forced to close the door on his true self, to become what they think he should be. Then there are the memories of those times when I look back and see myself wildly expressing my awe and wonder at life, being as emotional as I want to be, seeing then the envy in his face—the longing. And when I was violently whipped I saw the fear in his eyes. Surely, he must have felt that if Daddy could gather so much rage toward a girl out of her place, how much more rage could be summoned to direct at a boy failing to be what a boy should be.

These days my brother is still searching for fulfillment, doing the work of recovery, hoping to find again the soulful self he was forced to surrender long ago. He is still striving to be free and made whole. We search together, helping each other grow. We do the work of love.

When I first learned the story of Isis and Osiris, I heard this ancient Egyptian myth evoke a narrative of redemption and reunion, of healing from the trauma of loss and abandonment. It seemed a perfect archetypal African myth, uniquely suited to the experience of black males and females in the diaspora. In some versions of this myth Isis and Osiris are beloved sister and brother, in others wife and husband, and in still others simply soul mates. No matter their relationship they are bound together by ties of loving communion in mutual partnership. They are each other's fate.

In contemporary feminist re-visions of this mythic narrative Osiris is slaughtered by patriarchal enemies because of his disloyalty to dominator culture. His body is dismembered, cut up in pieces and spread far and wide. Isis grieves her loss then seeks reparation. She searches the world, collecting the bits and pieces of her partner's being, putting them together bit by bit until he is whole again. Jungian analyst James Hillman tells us to "imagine archetypes as the deepest patterns of psychic functioning, the roots of the soul governing the perspectives we have of ourselves and the world."

The story of Isis and Osiris offers a vision of healing that runs counter to the Western notion of individual healing, of the sick person alone doing the work to be well. It is a vision of healing that invites us to consider that a human being may be broken in some fundamental way that does not enable them to mend without healing intervention, without the help of loved ones. Isis is the loved one who knows her counterpart so well, she knows where the pieces fit. Like Six O says of the Thirty Mile woman in Toni Morrison's novel *Beloved* "she takes the bits and pieces that I am and gives them back to me in the right order." Insightfully dicussing the power of myth in *Shadow Dance: Liberating the Power of Creativity of Your Dark Side*, psychotherapist David Richo explains: "Isis re-membered Osiris, the resurrection god, by gathering the broken pieces of his body and creating the first mummy, the metaphor for the pupa that becomes a butterfly. It took forty days for the embalming to work. The embalming symbolizes the work it takes for transformation. . . ." Isis creates a context for Osiris to heal.

This myth provides a healing paradigm for black females and males who have suffered so long because of the myriad ways we are psychically "dismembered" in a culture of domination. It invites us to use our imaginations therapeutically, to take myth and re-vision it in our image. Certainly, when we consider the lot of black males in this nation at this critical time, when we face the crisis in black male spirit, we recognize that as intense suffering rends us, breaks our heart, it also breaks us open. In that revealed and exposed vulnerability lies the hope of reconciliation, renewal, and resurrection.

I have not given up on black men. And black men have not given up on me. At times black males have been the force in my life searching for me, laying hands on my broken spirit, helping me to choose salvation, helping me be whole. At times I have been Isis, there for my brothers, gathering the bits and pieces embracing their wholeness, loving them unconditionally.

This glorious myth, the tale of Isis and Osiris, reminds us that no matter how broken, how lost we are, we can be found. Our wounded souls are never beyond repair. Black females and males can use this myth to nurture the memory of sustained connection with one another, of a love that has stood and can stand the test of time and tribulation. We can choose a love that will courageously seek out the wounded soul, find you, and dare to bring you home again, doing what must be done to help put the bits and pieces together again, to make us whole. This is real cool. This is real love.